Training
Your
Children
To Turn Out
Right!

A Biblical Guide for Christian Parents

BY DAVID SORENSON

D1411469

AMERICAN ASSOCIATION OF CHRISTIAN SCHOOLS
P.O. BOX 2189 ♦ INDEPENDENCE, MO 64055

Published by
American Association of Christian Schools
P.O. Box 2189 ♦ Independence, MO 64055

ISBN 0-918-407-03-6

For my dear wife, Pam,
who lovingly supports
whatever I'm doing
and
has taught me much.

Acknowledgments

The Psalmist said, *"Thou hast given me the heritage of those that fear thy name."* I am humbled by the godly forebears God has privileged me to have. My dear parents have laid up for me a heritage for which I will be eternally thankful. Dad and Mother have spent over 50 years together in the gospel ministry. Without a doubt, their imprint is upon my life. They were preceded by my maternal grandparents who likewise spent approximately 50 years in the ministry of our Lord Jesus Christ. Grandma and Grandpa Lovik were not only a guide and influence upon my parents, but also upon me. Likewise, my paternal grandmother was a godly woman who profoundly influenced my father. Though these grandparents are now with the Lord, I must say, "Thank you Lord for such a godly heritage."

And how can I forget my dear wife, Pam, who has mothered our two sweet daughters. Her godly wisdom and encouragement has been an endless source of strength. Moreover, she has provided much of the impetus of this book. Though she is not trained academically in child psychology, nevertheless, she is a master of child psychology on a practical level. In addition, I must thank her for her efforts in the tedious chore of proof reading this book.

I also wish to thank Mrs. Julia Hansen, the AACS editor, who has spent many tedious hours putting this book into presentable form. She is a true professional. Additionally, I wish to thank the AACS editorial committee for deeming this book worthy of printing, and for Dr. Carl Herbster's input and for his part in writing the foreword.

David Sorenson *is a third-generation fundamental Baptist preacher. He attended Pillsbury Baptist Bible College and Central Baptist Theological Seminary in Minneapolis. He has been in the ministry since 1969. He has served as an assistant pastor in charge of the bus ministry in a large metropolitan church; as the associate pastor in his father's church in Pekin, Illinois, where he worked with the youth, bus ministry, and children' church; and senior pastor in three other churches in Minnesota and Florida. As a habit of life, he reads the Bible through seven times a year and the book of Proverbs every month.*

Pastor David Sorenson with his wife, Pam, and daughters, Heidi and Heather

Foreword

For several years, people have urged my wife and me to write a book on rearing children for the Lord, and I have put it off for many reasons. Now, however, David Sorenson has written the book instead of me. He has put into print much of what my wife and I tried to practice as we raised our three sons in the *"nurture and admonition of the Lord"* (Ephesians 6:4). The Biblical process works and has paid off in many spiritual benefits in the lives of our three sons. Pastor Sorenson attests to the fact that it has worked in the lives of his daughters as well. Our children as well as many others are living proof that God can and will work in the lives of our children if we are "training our children . . . right."

Please read every page of this book carefully. Reread and diligently study the principles from God's Word that are contained in this volume. However, merely reading and studying this book or even the Bible will not guarantee success in your children's lives. You must practice what is presented by Brother Sorenson if you want God's blessing (Joshua 1:8). Only then can you expect to see your children turn out "right" (Proverbs 22:6).

It will not always be easy and it will not always be fun, but the results are well worth the effort. Debbie and I know that there is no greater joy than to hear that our children walk in truth (II John 4). It is well said in Proverbs 23:24-25, *"The father of the righteous shall greatly rejoice: and he that begetteth a wise child shall have joy of him. Thy father and thy mother shall be glad, and she that bare thee shall rejoice."*

May God bless you and guide you as parents in the most important task given to you in God's Word, the training of your children. May God honor you with children who grow up to love and serve our Lord Jesus Christ. May God help you as you work at **"Training Your Children to Turn Out Right."**

Carl D. Herbster, 1995
Pastor, Tri-City Ministries
President, American Association of Christian Schools

Introduction

I think that I can say with some degree of certainty that Christian parents want to see their children become godly adults. It is seemingly a God-given instinct, particularly for born-again people. Few things touch the heart of a Christian parent more than his children and the desire to see the best for them.

As a pastor, my desire for the young people in our church is to see them turn out right. I am often concerned at seeing trends and practices in their lives that will produce other than God's best in them.

One of the joys of a pastor is to say as John said in II John 4, *"I rejoiced greatly that I found of thy children walking in truth."* Though that may be taking it slightly out of its context, it indeed is a joy to any pastor to see the young people in his church turn out right.

3

Conversely, it is a great burden for a pastor to see young people in his church wander into the world, drift into sin, and miss God's perfect will for their lives. Over the years, I have witnessed multitudes of seemingly Christian young people from Christian homes wind up deeply disappointing their parents, and in some cases breaking their parents' hearts. In my office deacons and their wives have sat across from me and literally *bawled* over what their son or daughter had done or was doing. I have taken phone calls from dedicated, faithful members of my church and heard their quivering voices say, "Pastor, I've got to talk to you about my kid. RIGHT NOW!"

I have watched children from Christian homes go off the deep end into sin and become prodigals. I have witnessed pastors or missionaries become discouraged because their children were a great heartache to them. In some cases, it has been the undoing of their ministry.

On the other hand, there are the wonderful stories of Christian young people who have kept themselves pure. There are many Christian young people who have developed genuine Christian character, given themselves to serve the Lord in a sacrificial full-time ministry, surrendered to preach, or have given their lives to serve the Lord on some foreign mission field. Then there are others who, though they may not be called of God to serve full-time in the ministry, nevertheless truly are an example of the believer in word, in conversation, in charity, in spirit, in faith, and in purity. What a blessing it is to see a completely dedicated, humble, pure, godly, disciplined Christian young person.

In talking with Christian parents, there is often the sense that bringing up a child in today's world is a big gamble. Maybe they will turn out right and maybe they will not. And sometimes there is the idea that, "Well, the devil got them, and there was nothing we could do." Both of those ideas are categorically wrong.

Chapter 1 - Gambling Is Prohibited

Training a child scripturally is not a gamble! Proper biblical training can fend off any attack that Satan may send.

Most Christian parents have weak guidelines for training their children. (I do not say that as a criticism, rather as an observation.) They draw from a mixture of what their parents did in training them, what the latest "pop" psychological advice is on rearing children, and what other parents are doing. Usually there is no strategy or well-defined goal.

The goal of even Christian child rearing often seems to be just to keep the child from getting into trouble like teenage pregnancy, involvement with drugs or alcohol, or having a record with the police. Christian parents who have this as their goal have the same underlying philosophy as the world. Not only is that philosophy fraught with error and danger, it will not prevent the very things it hoped to prevent. In fact, it may encourage such behavior.

The truth is, Christian parents must have an *active* goal and philosophy of training their children. If they lounge back and wait until trouble begins to develop, they have already made two major mistakes: (1) They have already waited too long and, (2) they probably have missed the opportunity to positively train their children to serve the Lord.

You see, God's goal for our children is not just for them to stay out of trouble. Rather, the emphasis throughout the Word of God is to train our children from their infancy to *serve* the Lord; to train them on purpose to be *righteous;* to train them specifically to be *godly;* to particularly train them to be *disciplined;* to train them to do the things they *ought to do;* to train them to *walk in the spirit.* The clear emphasis in the Word of God is not a negative *"thou shalt not."* Rather, it is positive. *"Train up a child in the way he should go, and when he is old, he will not depart from it"* (Proverbs 22:6).

The goal of every Christian parent ought to be that his children grow up to be *godly,* not just good. Anything less than that will be susceptible to the attack of the devil. The goal of every Christian parent needs to be to train his children to be *righteous* in every sense of the word, not just to keep them out of trouble. The goal of every Christian parent ought to be not only to see his children become Christians, but that they would become *servants of God.*

Old-fashioned Catholic families had a goal for at least one of their children to go into the priesthood or the convent. I wonder how many fundamental Christian parents have the goal to see at least one of their children go into the gospel ministry? I wonder how many actually train their entire family toward that end.

I would submit that the average Christian family has missed the boat in training their children. I am for Christian schools. My

6

children have gone through Christian schools of one form or another throughout their entire educational career. I wish the same for my grandchildren. But Christian schools, per se, and by themselves, may not turn out Christian young people dedicated to serving the Lord. Sadly, the history of the modern Christian school movement will bear that out.

Christian parents all across the nation have abdicated to the Christian school their God-given privilege and responsibility to train their own children in the way they should go. The Christian school can be a tremendous blessing, encouragement, and help to godly Christian parents seeking to train their children to serve the Lord. But by itself, it will not get the job done. God has given the responsibility of training children squarely and primarily to the parents. If the job of training our children does not get done right, Christian parents have no one to blame but themselves.

I am for youth programs, but youth programs, even in the church, will never instill godly character into our young people to the degree a godly parent can accomplish. They can help, but the job ultimately can only be done by Christian parents.

Athletics, per se, are not wrong, but athletics, even within a Christian context, will not cause a young person to serve God or develop righteous spiritual character. In the same way, keeping our kids busy so that they stay out of trouble is a false philosophy. Inevitably, Satan will lure them into the world and sin. There must be a positive, scriptural plan of training our young people.

Chapter 2 - The Firm Foundation

The longer I am in the ministry, the more I am critically aware of the necessity for born-again Christians to be in the Word of God 365 days a year. In fact, on several different occasions the Scripture speaks of being in the Word *day and night*. Somehow or other we have gotten the idea that the principle of being in the Word of God is for pastors, missionaries, and evangelists. It probably is a good idea for deacons, too, and it really would not hurt if every Christian would do that. "But, pastor, do you really expect kids to study the Word regularly? Isn't that getting a little radical? I mean, they aren't monks, are they?"

You may not fully grasp this, but we are touching on one of the *critical* keys that can, by itself, virtually guarantee that our children turn out right. As this book unfolds, you will find that the secret of training our children to turn out right is to train them to live a genuinely godly, spiritual, Christian life. That is impossible apart from the Word of God. Everything else in this book will be built upon that foundation—not only in principle but in practice.

The surest way to guarantee that your children turn out right is to see that they are in God's Word every single day. Yes, that should be 365 days a year, *day and night* throughout their formative years.

God spoke to Joshua 3400 years ago and instructed him, *"This book of the law shall not depart out of thy mouth; but thou shalt meditate therein day and night, that thou mayest observe to do according to all that is written therein: for then thou shalt make thy way prosperous, and then thou shalt have good success."* I know of no scriptural passage that abrogates that promise. As we shall see shortly, God reiterated it later. Let us briefly examine the principles and promises found in this portion of Scripture.

Day and Night

God instructed Joshua, among other things, to meditate in His Word day and night. To meditate is to reflect upon and think upon. It presumes that the individual is already aware of the text. Therefore, to meditate on the Word of God means, at the very least, to read it. We must read the Word before we can meditate upon it. We, as God's people, are to be a people who are in the Book daily.

Now, notice, God went a step further. Not only are we to go to the Word every day, but He charged Joshua to go to the Word *day and night.* I am not sure what the maximum implications of that injunction are, but, evidently, the minimum is to be in the Word at some point during the day and at some point in the evening. In day to day practice, that probably means being in the Word at the beginning of the day and at the end of the day. That is just the minimum. This is a blanket principle set forth in the Bible for all of God's people for all time. I believe it is intended for adults. I believe it also is intended for adolescents. I even believe it is within the scope of God's will for this to apply to children.

However, God did not finish there. Notice again in Joshua 1:8. God continued to instruct Joshua that he was to meditate therein day and night, **"that,"** or literally, **"so that"** he would observe to do **all** that is written therein. The point of going to the Word of God daily, and even day and night, is that we observe or come to actually **do** what it says.

Years ago, my wife and I decided that we would do anything that would help our children spiritually. We were aware of how Satan lays clever traps for Christian young people through the world and the flesh. The *one* thing that will give them clear victory is the Word of God. That was true in Joshua's day and it is still true today.

Over the years, I have come to understand Psalm 119:11 a bit differently than perhaps is the conventional understanding. The Holy Spirit inspired David to write *"Thy word have I hid in mine heart, that I might not sin against thee."* I do not believe this is a reference to rote memorization. However, I believe that the thought is to so fill our minds with God's Word that it soaks down into our hearts and begins to affect every decision we make. The result is that we *will not* sin against God.

Now, that is an extension of the principle of Joshua 1:8. When we fill our minds with God's Word by meditating therein day and night, it will soak down into our hearts. The result is that we begin to actually do what God in His Word has said to do. On the one hand, so doing will keep God's people from sin. On the other hand, it will predispose us to do what is right.

God's Success System

God went on to tell Joshua in Joshua 1:8 that if he would meditate in His Word day and night to the point that he actually did all that God had written, **then** He would make his way *prosperous*, and **then** he would have good *success*. Now, I do not know about you, but that sounds like a good deal to me. I hope to be prosperous and have good success. I wish that even more for my children.

Over 400 years later, the Holy Spirit inspired David to write a similar thought in Psalm 1. *"Blessed is the man that walketh not in the counsel of the ungodly, nor standeth in the way of sinners, nor sitteth in the seat of the scornful. But His delight is in the law of the Lord; and in his law doth he meditate day and night. And he shall be like a tree planted by the rivers of water, that bringeth forth his fruit in his season; his leaf also shall not wither; and whatsoever he doeth shall prosper."* Psalm 1:1-3 is a divinely inspired commentary upon Joshua 1:8. Verse one essentially says to *get out of* the world, and verse two essentially says to *get into* the Word of God.

Notice again, there is the concept of meditating in God's Word day and night. Verses 1-3 of Psalm 1 are a whole, but let us focus at this time on just verses two and three. Notice, the man that God will bless will (a) delight in the law of the Lord (i.e., His Word), and (b) meditate therein *day and night.*

Notice also how meditating affects and influences people. First, they will have strength and stability in life like a tree. In the realm of nature no type of plant has greater strength, stability, and longevity than a tree. Furthermore, if that tree happens to be planted by a river, it will increasingly flourish. Its leaves will not wither and it will bear fruit.

The Psalmist takes the analogy of a tree a step further. The individual who delights in God's Word and meditates therein day and night shall prosper in whatever he does. That is not *my* idea. That is from the Word of God.

If this principle and promise apply to adults, then they will as much, if not more, apply to children. It is imperative that we begin at the earliest possible time to develop this practice in our children if we want them to turn out right. Perhaps I sound dogmatic. But I believe if Christian parents will instill the practice of having their children go to God's Word *day and night*, 365 days a year, from the time they learn to read until the time they leave home, they will have helped their children beyond measure.

Christian parents must model this practice themselves, but often do not. It may be they have never really understood this wonderful promise and principle in the Word of God. Nevertheless, it is there for anyone to read. It has been there for thousands of years, and it applies as much to parents as it does to children.

Parents, you will have a difficult time leading your children down a path where you have never gone. But your Christian life can be revolutionized by the simple, age-old practice of going to the Word of God to read and meditate day and night.

Let us look at more Scripture. Psalm 119:1-3 says, *"Blessed are the undefiled in the way, who walk in the law of the Lord. Blessed are they that keep his testimonies, and that seek him with the whole heart. They also do no iniquity: they walk in his ways."*

Notice that those who walk in the law of the Lord will be undefiled. That means those who walk in the law of the Lord will not be defiled or corrupted by sin. Here is God's preventive principle. To walk in the law of the Lord first requires that the individual **be** in the law of the Lord. That means to spend time reading and studying it.

Then, verse two speaks of keeping or obeying His Word and seeking him with the whole heart. Notice the result in verse

13

three—*"they also do no iniquity."* The word "iniquity" in the Old Testament is a word relating to willful or rebellious sin. Here is the key to preventing adolescent rebellion. Get your children into the Word of God and the younger the better.

I know you are saying, "Well, that's easier said than done." I know, and we will spend some time on that shortly. Let me just say this now: the earlier you begin your children on a schedule of getting into God's Word every single day, the easier it will be. The later in life you wait, the more difficult it will be. (We began having our girls read very limited portions of God's Word while they were still in kindergarten.)

Let us go even further. Psalm 119:9 says, *"Wherewithal shall a young man cleanse his way? by taking heed thereto according to thy word."* Again, we find the biblical principle of God's Word in the life of a young person cleansing his way of life. (The principle is true for older people as well.) Christian parents have somehow gotten the idea that the Bible is too boring, too heavy, or too deep for children and adolescents to read. Therefore, in our finite wisdom, we have tried to come up with a better way than God's way.

We rush out and get the latest book on how to raise children by some behavioral psychologist, or we try to get our children involved in all kinds of activities and programs hoping that collectively they will help our children to turn out right. Is it plausible to think that God in His infinite wisdom might have a simpler and better solution?

Solomon repeatedly admonished his son to receive God's Word and hide His commandments with him. He urged his son not to forget His law nor His commandments. Dear parent, we are touching upon one of the most basic ways in which we are to train up our children. In His Word God repeatedly admonishes *all* of His people to study to show themselves approved unto God; to give attendance to reading; to meditate in His Word day and night; to walk in the law of the Lord.

It is the conviction and thesis of this author that this principle extends to our children as well. Furthermore, I believe one reason there has been such a declension in Christian young people is that we have forgotten this God-given, age-old principle. This principle is so simple!

Developing the Habit

Dear parents, the most important habit you will ever teach your children is the habit of going to the Word of God day and night. You will notice that I used the word "habit." That is on purpose. This matter of going to the Word of God is something that must be developed as a habit.

Habits are developed through repetitive actions, but for children to develop the habit of going to the Bible each day, you, the parents, must take steps to insert this practice into the lives of your children. You cannot just tell them to do it and expect them to follow through. You must set up a program, a schedule, and incentives to help motivate them to be in the Book. When a given practice is enforced day after day after day, month after month, year after year, it will become a habit.

Over the years, I have had people say, "Well, I think we should read the Bible because we *want* to, not because we *have* to." Between the world, the flesh, and the devil, there will be many more days that we do not feel like getting into the Word than days in which we want to. Anytime we do what we do simply because we feel like it or want to, we are living a very shallow life spiritually. However, we should read God's Word because we ought to, because it is right, and because it is God's will. How we feel about it on a given day is irrelevant. What our flesh may want on a given day is folly. God said to do it, therefore, we will do it. We also need to instill that attitude and philosophy into our children.

15

Dear parent, the way your children will ever adopt such a practice and habit into their lives is by you, the parent, insisting upon it. **You** must plan it, you must enforce it, and you must police it. No one else will ever so effectually accomplish this in the lives of your children, especially while they are young. The Christian school teacher probably will not insist on such. Even if he or she did, they will never be as effective in developing and enforcing such a practice as you the parent. The youth leaders in your church may or may not encourage such a habit, but only you, the parent, can really develop such a habit in your children. Do not allow such a critically important practice to be given to another. Do it yourself.

There is no question in my mind that you will ever instill a more important concept into the lives of your children than the concept of going to the Word of God, day and night, 365 days a year, for the rest of their lives. Christian parents insist that their children brush their teeth regularly, even multiple times a day. They will make their children do whatever homework is required. They will require that they properly bathe. They will plan meals so that they eat as they ought, but why will they not see to it that their children adopt a spiritual practice that will have a positive impact for the rest of their lives? God has specifically promised to bless, prosper, and protect those who do.

Some may be saying, "Well, what profit is it if they don't understand what they are reading? Won't they get bored and rebel?" Few adults totally understand all of what they read in the Word of God. That is not the point. God's Word has an intrinsic cleansing property to it. It is miraculous spiritually. *"Wherewithal shall a young man cleanse his way? by taking heed thereto according to thy word."* The Scriptures will cleanse our children spiritually. It is like running water through a strainer. The water passes right through it, but in so doing, it tends to cleanse it. Moreover, if a parent wisely administers such a program, it need not be boring nor spur rebellion.

16

Practical Tips

Let us look at some practical tips on how to instill this practice into our children.

1. **Start early.** Our children learned to read in a rudimentary fashion near the end of their kindergarten year in the Christian school. We, therefore, sat them down respectively and explained how important it was to begin to read God's Word each day. We explained that as they read God would help them and bless their lives. We explained to them that it was exciting to read God's Word each day and that we were going to help them start to do it in their lives. They became excited about the idea. We made a big deal about it as they began to read where we directed them.

2. **Plan their reading.** The Bible is a complex book. It is a library of 66 different books. Many books are complicated, especially for a child. Some biblical books have vocabulary even moderate readers struggle with. One of the simplest books in the Bible with regard to vocabulary and syntax is the book of I John. This is where children should begin to read each day.

When we started our girls into their daily Bible reading plan we placed a book mark at I John 1. When they first began, we set a goal for them to read one verse in the morning and then one verse in the evening. Initially, we did the reading with them and helped them with it. They were excited to know that they had read out of the Bible on their very own. We then showed them how to put a little mark at the end of the verse so that when they came back the next time, they could easily pick up where they left off.

As they progressed in their reading, we increased the goal to three verses a day in their first grade year. As they progressed even further in their reading ability, they went to five verses a day, then eight verses a day. In about third or fourth grade, they began to read a chapter a day. When they became sixth-graders they were to read two chapters a day, one in the morning and one in the evening. When they reached junior high school, they went to reading four chapters a day. This basically will take anyone through the Bible in a year. That regimen continued throughout their high school years.

3. **Provide positive incentive.** When our girls were small, my wife made a little chart and placed it on the refrigerator. Each morning when they did their prescribed Bible reading, we placed a colored star on the chart. When they did their evening reading, they also received a star. The idea was to fill every day of the week with two stars. As each week passed by, we made a big production about the fact that they had all the places on their charts filled with stars.

If you have never implemented the practice of regular Bible reading in your home, and your children are older, the star idea may need to be modified. Initially, you may want to add an incentive, like some special treat, for having a chart completed for a month or whatever time frame you decide. Do address the matter in a positive fashion. Explain how important it is. Tell how God has promised to bless them, and then give some external incentive or reward in the initial phase of developing the habit.

One of the greatest and most effective means of training our children is by example. I did my own personal Bible reading before breakfast and often right after supper. As a result, our children saw their father doing exactly what he was teaching them to do, and that was a major reenforcement of the principle to them. More is caught than is taught in training children.

However, my wife usually did her personal Bible reading after the children went to school and after they went to bed. Therefore, they rarely saw their mother reading the Word. One day, one of the children came to her and said, "Mommy, how come you never read *your* Bible?" Pam was taken aback until she realized that the children never saw her read. She carefully explained to them about her schedule. Furthermore, after that

Chapter 3 - The Right Way to Grow

It has been aptly said, "That which is profound is usually simple." We come to another profound principle that is as simple as it is important. Isaiah 61:3 says, *"that they might be called trees of righteousness, the planting of the LORD, that he might be glorified."* Though the context of this passage of Scripture is of Christ and the millennium, I believe we do it no injustice to apply it to our children. Oh, that it might be said that our children were *"trees of righteousness, the planting of the LORD, that He might be glorified."*

As I look out my office window towards the woods at the edge of the yard, there are many types of plants visible. There are various types of grasses. There are a variety of wild shrubs and bushes growing, but what is most noticeable are the birch, aspen, and maple trees as far as the eye can see. They tower over the shrubs, weeds, and bushes beneath them. They live many times longer than the underbrush. They are strong and resilient, and for the most part, they grow straight toward the sky. Their value in a variety of ways is immense.

People do not come onto our property and remark about the beauty of the weeds or comment about the value of the underbrush, but they frequently comment about the distinctive beauty of the trees. Not only are they aesthetically beautiful, they could conceivably be used for valuable lumber. They could theoretically be used to make furniture or cabinets. The straighter they are, the more valuable they become. Underbrush, weeds, and scrub bushes have no such value. There is something about a tree.

When our children were small, this portion of Scripture struck me as a guide for their training: to so train and mold them that they would someday become trees of righteousness. That has been one of the guiding principles we have followed during their upbringing.

Biblical Righteousness

The Bible fairly overflows with the concept of righteousness. At one point, years ago, I got out my concordance and counted all the references in the Bible that pertained to "righteousness, uprightness, just, justly, right, righteous," etc. (and other words used in the original Greek or Hebrew that were similarly translated). To my amazement I found that this concept appears more than 1,300 times in the Scripture. The book of Psalms and Proverbs abound with it.

Much in the Scripture relates to righteousness. One aspect of our salvation is called justification, which means being declared righteous. Wisdom is equated with righteousness in Proverbs. Most of the kings of Judah and of Israel were categorized by the simple statement, "He did that which was right in the sight of the Lord" or, "He did not that which was right in the sight of the Lord." The Lord Jesus Christ is referred to as *"Jesus Christ the Righteous,"* and as the *"righteous Judge."*

Throughout the Old Testament, God the Father is referred to as righteous. God's Word is referred to on several occasion as *"thy righteous commandments."* As New Testament Christians we are admonished to *"follow after righteousness"* and that we *"should live unto righteousness"* (I Peter 2:25).

I have traced other concepts and topics through the Scripture, and though my research on those words certainly is incomplete, I have come to this conclusion: I am not aware of another ethical or moral precept in the Bible that is mentioned more than righteousness. It seemingly is the moral and ethical essence of Christian character.

It may be well to explain at this point that there are basically two types of righteousness referred to in the Bible. In the New Testament, those who are saved are referred to as "righteous". One facet of our salvation accordingly is called justification. Indeed, we have been justified. (The term "just" is identical to the term "righteous".) Therefore, the term "justification" literally means to be declared righteous, and "justified" literally means one who has been declared righteous. The two terms (righteous and just) are identical in both the Hebrew and Greek. (The only difference is that the translators chose to use different English words, perhaps for variety.) We might refer to this type of righteousness as *positional righteousness*.

However, in the Old Testament the term "righteous" and its derivations refer most frequently to doing what is right *practically.* That concept is used somewhat in the New Testament as well. Therefore, the alternative sense is of *practical righteousness.*

The vast majority of references to righteousness in the Bible refer to practical righteousness. It is the simple matter of *doing* that which is ethically and morally right. Righteousness, in its most basic concept, is obeying God. Anytime we do what God has said to do, it is right.

Because righteousness is so dominant as a principle in the Bible, it must be very important. I believe it is a critical principle needed in the training of godly young people. We will now take an overview of the concept in the Scripture.

David prayed as Solomon was about to ascend the throne, *"I know also, my God, that thou triest the heart, and hast pleasure in uprightness"* (I Chronicles 29:17). Simply put, David knew that God takes pleasure when His people do what is right.

David prayed elsewhere, *"Lead me, O LORD, in thy righteousness . . . "* (Psalm 5:8). Then at the end of that chapter he cried, *"For thou, LORD, wilt bless the righteous; with favor wilt thou compass him as with a shield"* (Psalm 5:12). God's Word has promised to bless those who live righteously. He will surround them with favor as with a shield.

Remember Job? Job 1:1 says he was upright. A frustrated devil reminded God in Job 1:10 that God had *"made an hedge about him, and about his house, and about all that he hath on every side? thou has blessed the work of his hands, and his substance is increased in the land."* God had blessed righteous Job. And with favor he had compassed him as with a shield. Though God allowed Job to be tested, God returned his blessing to him and, in fact, doubled it.

Psalm 11:7 says, *"For the righteous LORD loveth righteousness; his countenance doth behold the upright."* Two things are clear: (1) God loves righteousness; and (2) He watches over the upright. The Psalmist wrote in Psalm 33:5, *"He loveth righteousness and judgment."* In Jeremiah we read, *"that I am the LORD which exercise lovingkindness, judgment, and righteousness, in the earth: **for in these things I delight,** saith the LORD"* (Jeremiah 9:24). Take note that one of the things that the Lord delights in upon the earth is righteousness.

Psalm 45 is one of the great Messianic Psalms. The Psalmist here wrote of the Messiah seated upon His throne in the millennium. In verse seven of this Psalm, David said in reference to Jesus Christ, *"Thou lovest righteousness, and hatest wickedness: therefore God, thy God, hath anointed thee with the oil of gladness above thy fellows."* When the author of Hebrews was inspired of the Holy Spirit to write a commentary on Psalm 45 more than a thousand years later, he went on to say that *"a sceptre of righteousness is the sceptre of thy kingdom."* It is evident from this passage that Jesus Christ, the Messiah, loves righteousness and that God the Father has anointed Him because of it. Furthermore, the very character of His kingdom will be in righteousness. The prophet Isaiah wrote, speaking of Christ in the millennium, *"But with righteousness shall he judge the poor. . . and righteousness shall be the girdle of his loins . . . "* (Isaiah 11:4,5). Everything about Jesus Christ is righteous. The Apostle John referred to him as *"Jesus Christ the righteous"* in I John 2:1. In II Timothy 4:8, he is called the *"righteous judge"*.

The Psalmist wrote in Psalm 106:3, *"Blessed are they that keep judgment, and he that doeth righteousness at all times."* The word "judgment" here is in the sense of "right judgment". Again, the promise is found in God's Word that those who live and do righteousness will be blessed. God promised in Psalm 112:2 that, *"the generation of the upright shall be blessed."* He promised in Psalm 84:11 that, *"no good thing will he withhold from them that walk uprightly."* In Psalms 146:8 we read, *"the LORD loveth the righteous."*

It seems rather clear that: (1) God loves righteousness; (2) God has promised to bless those who live uprightly; and (3) Jesus Christ is righteous in His personal character. As we train our children to be Christ-like, here is one major principle.

That is not all. Righteousness is a basis for answered prayer. In Psalm 34:15 the Word of God says, *"The eyes of the LORD are upon the righteous, and his ears are open unto their cry."*

That passage is quoted again in I Peter 3:12. Proverbs 15:8 says that *"the prayer of the upright is his delight."* Later in that same chapter we read, *"but he heareth the prayer of the righteous" (29).* And again in Proverbs 15:9, we read, *"He loveth him that followeth after righteousness."* We read in Proverbs 2:7 that *"he is a buckler to them that walk uprightly."* (God protects the upright.) Again, *"He blesseth the habitation of the just"* (Proverbs 3:33). In Proverbs 8 righteousness is essentially equated with wisdom and vice versa.

In the New Testament, we are instructed to *"follow after righteousness,"* and *"live unto righteousness."* When Jesus Christ returns at the battle of Armageddon, we are told in Revelation 19:11 that *"in righteousness he doth judge and make war."*

II Chronicles (as well as much of I and II Kings) are divinely inspired biographies and epithets of the kings of Judah and Israel. What is interesting is that God described many of those kings in terms of whether they did right or not.

Here are some examples. In II Chronicles 14:2 we read that, *"Asa did that which was good and right in the eyes of the LORD his God."* In II Chronicles 24:2 we read that, *"Joash did that which was right in the sight of the LORD all the days of Jehoiada the priest."* Likewise, Amaziah *"did that which was right in the sight of the LORD, but not with a perfect heart"* (II Chronicles 25:2). Uzziah *"did that which was right in the sight of the LORD according to all that his father . . . did"* (II Chronicles 26:4). However, Ahaz *"did not that which was right in the sight of the LORD, like David his father"* (II Chronicles 28:1). In contrast Hezekiah *"did that which was right in the sight of the LORD, according to all that David his father had done"* (II Chronicles 29:2).

Josiah, one of the great kings of Judah, began to reign when he was eight years old. And God said, *"he did that which was right in the sight of the LORD, and walked in the ways of David his father, and declined neither to the right hand or to the left"*

(II Chronicles 34:2). Likewise, Jehoshaphat was characterized as walking in the ways of Asa his father, *"doing that which was right in the eyes of the LORD" (I Kings 22:43).*

"Jehoash did that which was right in the sight of the LORD all his days wherein Jehoiada the priest instructed him" (II Kings 12:2). Moreover, Amaziah *"did that which was right in the sight of the LORD, yet not like David his father"* (II Kings 14:3). Furthermore, Jotham *"did that which was right in the sight of the LORD"* (II Kings 15:34). In addition, many of these kings are mentioned more than once in the dual histories in Kings and Chronicles.

It is no coincidence that God chose to memorialize these kings in terms of whether they did right or not. That description well summarizes how they lived their lives before God, and God took note of it. How will God characterize the lives of our children someday? Would to God it will be said that our children did that which was right in the sight of the Lord all the days of their lives.

Of course, our ultimate righteousness is in Jesus Christ. There is no person who is completely righteous apart from Him. God spoke about these Jewish leaders mentioned above in relative terms. In the main these men did that which was right throughout their lives. Here is a pattern and goal for the training of our children.

This is just a summary of the concept in the Bible. Literally hundreds and hundreds of other references refer to this principle, but it should be obvious from this cursory overview that righteousness is part of the very essence of the nature and character of Jesus Christ. He delights in it. He has promised to bless and protect those who walk uprightly.

Now then, let us apply this to the training of our children. If we would train our children to be Christ-like, we must of necessity implant into them the principle of righteousness. I believe in so doing we will not only please God, but also we will

27

do our children a tremendous favor by instilling into them the *habit* of always doing what is right. When our children have learned this principle and developed it in their lives, most other areas of training and spiritual development will follow rather easily.

Like any other proper habit, doing right is learned by repetitive action. As we encourage and urge our children to practice doing what is right, in due season it will become a habit. Therefore, the more the doing of right is talked about and practiced, the greater the chance of it becoming a habit.

For example, the classic admonition in Ephesians 6:1, of teaching children to obey their parents, is followed with the qualification, *"for this is right."* When children have learned to accept the concept of righteousness, it only makes sense to obey their parents. Why? It's right! Simple, isn't it?

Likewise, it is right to read the Bible. Therefore, the matter developed in the preceding chapter has added impetus to it. It is right. Therefore, we must do it. "Is it right to be kind to each other?" Indeed! Therefore, we must do it. "Is it right to be respectful to one's mother and father?" Indeed! Therefore, we will do it. As a child grows into adolescence, the question may be asked, "Is it right to be morally pure?" Indeed! Therefore, we will be pure. And the list can go on and on. If something is right, then we must do it.

Instilling Righteousness

Let's look at four ways to instill the concept of righteousness into the warp and woof of the character of our children.

1. Teach righteousness as a precept. That is, teach it directly. Over the years, as our children were growing up and especially when they were young, we taught them, "We always do what's right!" If they heard that once, they heard it a thousand times, especially in their preschool years. Every day, over and over again, we taught them, "We always do what's right." "We always do what's right." Little by little our children got the idea they always were to do what is right. Did they always do what was right? No. But they began to be predisposed to that conviction.

In our daily family devotions we would frequently go to one of the many references to righteousness in the Bible and make it the general topic of our devotions that day. For example, we might focus on Psalm 5:12 where the Scripture says, *"For thou LORD wilt bless the righteous; with favor wilt thou compass him as with a shield."*

We would talk about who it was in this verse that God promised to bless, or we would talk about who it was that God would favor or shield. On other days we might talk about specific applications of doing right such as obedience or being helpful, etc. We might go to Proverbs and look at the myriad of references to righteousness there. Each day we would pick one verse and talk about it.

You might comment that after a year or so, if not sooner, we would run out of such material. That is true, at least for simple day to day family devotions, and we did indeed deal with other matters in our family devotions. However, we would usually come back and repeat the basic principles after a period of time. On the one hand, repetition is the mother of learning. On the other hand, as they grew older, we felt a need to apply the principle of righteousness to the needs and problems they faced with each ensuing year.

Children, by their very nature, tend to do what they do because they *want to* or *do not want to.* They tend to be motivated by what is fun or what is not fun. Though that is as natural as the old nature they were born with, we need to instill in them a higher and more spiritual motive. Rather than doing what they want to do, teach your children to do what they ought to do.

29

Doing what we ought is essentially doing what is right. If it is right, than we ought to do it. And if we ought to do it, then it most likely is right. We need to teach our children that there is a better and higher way of living than doing what we want or do not want to do. That principle is doing what we ought to do or what is right.

Virtually every child to ever breathe has complained to their parents, "Awe mom, I don't *want* to." We need to teach our children that that is beside the point. If it is right or if it is something we ought to do, then that settles it. We do it. A similar refrain heard by virtually every parent is, "But Dad, that isn't any fun." Again, that is beside the point. If it is right or if we ought to do it, that settles it. We will do it, period.

So much of our modern culture is based upon the fun motive. "I mean, we were just trying to have a little fun." Fun, per se, is not wrong. A philosophy of life based upon having fun is not only shallow, but it is also dangerous. As children grow into adolescence, doing something because it is supposed to be fun can lead to tragic results. Whether it is the alleged fun of drinking, or the potential fun of illicit sex, or the fun of just hot rodding around, fun can get a young person into a lot of trouble.

A major antidote to that unscriptural philosophy is rooting the philosophy of righteousness into the lives of our children long before they reach the crucial teenage years. Righteousness is indeed a buckler and a shield to them that walk uprightly. It will keep them out of a heap of trouble.

The standard and source of righteousness are found in the Word of God. As we train our children to be in the Book each day, the principle of righteousness will be continually reenforced. Furthermore, the standards of right and wrong are clearly defined in the Scripture. Therefore, the reading and studying of the Bible complements the concept of doing what is right.

We learn of right as a principle in the Bible. We also learn exactly *what* is right therein. I once had a lady in all sincerity say

30

to me, "But pastor, how can I know what is right?" My answer was simply, "Go to the Word of God. It is the ultimate source of what is right."

2. Apply the principle of righteousness. This is a corollary to the preceding idea and we have already touched upon it in passing. Our children needed to know not only the principle of righteousness, but also the practical outworking of it. Therefore, we would think of all of the things our children needed to do or not do and relate it to the principle of righteousness.

For example, as mentioned above, it is only natural and convenient to begin with the admonition of obedience to parents *"for this is right."* We would teach our children that rock and roll music was not *right*. We would teach them that smoking was not only bad, it was not *right*. It was *right* to tell the truth. And, it was not *right* to lie. We taught our children that evolution was not *right*. Treating your sister kindly was *right*. It was *right* to clean your room. It was *right* to be on time. It was *right* to read the Bible. It was *right* to pray. It was *right* to obey the rules at school. It was not *right* to have a bad attitude. It was not *right* to be selfish. It was not *right* to steal. And we could go on and on.

Virtually any child can understand the basic principle of right and wrong. Relating basic standards of conduct to the simple matter of doing what is right greatly simplifies a child's understanding of what is expected. More than that, the entire matter of conduct and attitude is tied directly to the basic biblical precept of doing what is right. Teach it over and over again.

3. Teach righteousness by example. It is axiomatic that as much is caught as is taught. Our talk talks, and our walk talks; but our walk talks louder than our talk talks. Truly, what we do speaks louder than what we say. Inconsistency on the part of a parent will do more to breed rebellion than virtually any other matter, and conversely, a consistent example will do more to reenforce what we say than just about anything else.

If we teach our children that it is right to read their Bible, then we had better let them see us reading our Bible. I will never forget how an eight-year-old boy in our church one day proudly told of how he watched his daddy reading his Bible early in the morning. I suspect that father did not have a hard time teaching his son to do the same thing.

If we teach our children that it is right to be faithful in attendance to church services, then we had better do the same, even when fishing season opens, and when hunting season opens, and when we are on vacation. If we teach our children that certain types of TV programming are not right, woe be to us if they catch us watching the same after they go to bed.

If we teach them it is not right to cheat, but then they find out we cheated on our tax returns or in some other way, we will have unraveled much of what we have sought to instill in them. In fact, we will have done worse than neutralize our counsel. We may well encourage rebellion and a cynical attitude.

You will teach few things more forcefully than by the example you set. If you reenforce righteous living by your example, that example will powerfully strengthen the same concept in your children, but if you are not consistent in what you teach, woe be to you. You are sowing the seeds of rebellion, and they will grow.

Tragically, parental inconsistency can breed not only rebellion against the parent, but against the Lord. As parents, we stand in God's place and are His representatives to our children. When children see us being inconsistent, it not only causes them to be disappointed in us, but also in the God we represent.

4. Teach righteousness early and long. As soon as your children are able to understand speech, begin to instill the principle of right. Continue it on through their adolescent years. Not only will you help instill the essence of Christian character, but you also will put them in a place where God can bless them.

An interesting corollary in the Scripture is that righteousness and wisdom are very closely related. In fact, the concept of wisdom and righteousness in the Bible are used almost synonymously in portions of the book of Proverbs.

Notice how that in Proverbs 8:1-6 wisdom is personified. *"Doth not wisdom cry? . . . She standeth in the top of high places . . . She crieth at the gates . . . . Hear; for I will speak of excellent things; and the opening of my lips shall be right things."* Then notice in Proverbs 8:8 how that wisdom personified says, *"All the words of my mouth are in righteousness."* And then notice also in Proverbs 8:20 how that wisdom says, *"I lead in the way of righteousness."*

When one pauses to reflect upon the matter, it becomes evident that when we do what is right we have also done what is wise. And conversely, when we have done what is wise, we will have done what is right. It is indisputable. Wisdom and righteousness are so closely interrelated that they are almost one and the same. To be wise is to do what is right. And to do what is right is to be wise.

When this concept is coupled with the injunction in Proverbs 4, concerning the importance of wisdom, it gives added significance to the matter of righteousness. Notice in Proverbs 4:5-7, the Word of God says, *"Get wisdom, get understanding: forget it not; neither decline from the words of my mouth. Forsake her [wisdom] not, and she shall preserve thee: love her, and she shall keep thee. Wisdom is the principal thing; therefore get wisdom: and with all thy getting get understanding."*

We will not take the time at this point to further embellish this correlation, but it is interesting how wisdom is called the principal thing, and we are to seek it. The greater overview of Proverbs is of Solomon, a wise father, seeking to impart wisdom to his son.

So, in summary, teach righteousness in your home. Make it a permeating principle during the children's formative years. Seek to weave into the very warp and woof of their character the matter of always doing what is right.

God has promised to bless the righteous. I long for God's blessing on my children. Consequently, I must train them to be righteous. God has promised to protect the righteous. I long to see God's protective care upon my children. Therefore, I must train them to be righteous. God has promised to answer the prayer of the righteous. Therefore, I must train my children to be righteous so that they may have that privilege.

As we will see in a coming chapter, the essence of Christian character is the self-discipline to do what is right. If I would have my children develop Christian character, therefore, I must train them in the principle of righteousness. That is, I must train them to always do what is right. I have appreciated the conviction of Dr. Bob Jones, Sr., in his saying, "Do right till the stars fall." Majesty Music has put those words to music in the song, "Do Right":*

> *Do right till the stars fall,*
> *Do right till the last call,*
> *Do right though no one stands with you.*
> *Do right when you're all alone.*
> *Do right though it's never known.*
> *Do right since you love the LORD,*
> *Do right, do right!*

*Used by permission: Majesty Music, Greenville, S.C.

Chapter 4 - Directing Through Discipline

Hudson Taylor once said, "An undisciplined person will never amount to anything in God's work." I would certainly agree. In fact, I will go a step further. An undisciplined person will likely never amount to much in any area of life.

To some, the term "discipline" has a negative connotation. To these, it implies severity, strictness, and perhaps punitive measures. There are really few things more positive than discipline. It certainly needs to be a major factor in the training of Christian children.

Discipline is a major factor in the two principles already discussed—daily study of God's Word and doing what is right. The key to accomplishing both of those principles is self-discipline. Notice that in the last sentence a modifying word was added: *self*-discipline. As we develop this marvelous concept in this chapter, we will at times use the shorter term "discipline," but in most cases the greater sense of self-discipline will be what is meant.

Self-discipline

Self-discipline is the key to success in virtually all areas of life. If spirituality might be related to time spent in the Word of God and prayer, then the undergirding principle is self-discipline. In the long run, we will not effectively stay in the Word or prayer without self-discipline.

As we will see later, self-discipline is a major factor in the matter of Christian character. An undisciplined person, as a rule, will not have a high degree of character. That may sound harsh and judgmental, but I believe it is true.

A major key to education is self-discipline. Discipline is important in the matter of proper behavior so that attention is held. More importantly, the imposing of discipline, and ultimately self-discipline, upon the mind is a secret to ongoing education.

Self-discipline is the key to punctuality. It is the secret to being organized, and it is the main ingredient to neatness. It will greatly expand productivity in a work context. It is a major ingredient in emotional strength and stability. It also is a profound factor in something so commonplace as weight control. If these be so, it would appear that self-discipline is very important. And it is. Without it, every principle in this book will be a struggle, if not impossible to accomplish.

Incidentally, the matter of self-discipline is just as crucial for adults as it is for children. The reason so many children are not self-disciplined, or disciplined at all, lies in the fact that their parents never have learned to be disciplined. Curiously, disciplined children tend to come from several generations of disciplined parents and grandparents. Likewise, undisciplined children tend to have several generations of undisciplined forebears.

As a pastor, I have witnessed families of four generations within the church. Interestingly, the traits of discipline or the lack thereof tend to be passed from generation to generation. I do not believe this is genetic or biological. Rather, it is acquired habits and patterns of life that each generation tends to pick up from the previous one. Again, as much is caught as is taught.

We as adults need to examine our lives and see just how disciplined we really are. We will tend to pass on to our children the degree of self-discipline we have achieved in our lives. However, the good news is that we as parents can always lift our own level of self-discipline. Habits of life are not easy to change, but with God's help we can do what is right. Self-discipline certainly is right, and it is far better to train discipline into the lives of our children from the very first.

I will never forget a situation in which one of the men of the church came to me distraught. One of his teenage children was in the process of going off the deep end into sin. In the course of events that child proceeded to break the hearts of both parents. However, in the poignant conversation that particular day, this fine Christian man revealed to me that he and his wife had never forced their children to do anything they did not want to do.

It was not the time to say, "Well, your chickens are coming home to roost," but that is exactly what was happening. They as parents at some point had picked up one of the prevailing fads of child psychology: do not force your children to do what they do not want to do.

Those good people had failed to implant any significant degree of discipline into their children, and the harvest was starting to come in. I am convinced that had the principle of discipline been woven into the lives of those children while their hearts were tender, the results would have been far different in the late

37

adolescent years. If only the parents had instilled in them the concept of "doing what we ought rather than what we want, even if we do not like it" things may have been different.

Discipline or Disorders?

I make no pretense of being a psychologist. However, I am convinced that much of what is diagnosed by modern child psychologists is just a figment of their professional imagination. It seems that decade by decade and almost year by year new "psychological" disorders are "discovered" in children. I have spent the past 25 years in the ministry dealing with people as well as studying the Word of God. I am convinced that some of these "disorders" are things that psychologists have invented to describe children who are just lacking in self-discipline.

In the earlier years of our ministry, my wife and I worked with large numbers of children in various children's church and youth programs. My wife, particularly, has worked with children for over 27 years and in my estimation is a master in working with them. I have watched her literally command children's meetings in which there were over 700 children present. For years, we routinely worked in children's church services with 300 children present every week. A large percentage of these children came from the Sunday School bus routes.

"Bus kids," generally come from lower income and frequently troubled homes. There seems to be a disproportionately high percentage of children in this category who have been "diagnosed" by school psychologists or social workers as hyperactive, learning disabled, or having an attention deficit disorder. And indeed, these children tended to be disorderly.

In later years as the nature of our ministry changed, Pam has continued to work with children. Though the group size she has worked with in more recent years is smaller, parents still come to her and tell her that "Johnny" is hyperactive, or "Susie" has an attention deficit disorder, or little "Billy" is learning disabled. Our experience usually has been that these children have had very little encouragement in self-discipline. They have ants in their pants not only because their diet may be rich in sugar and caffeine, but more importantly, no one has ever taken the time and *effort* to instill discipline in them.

I have watched Pam work with children who are "hyperactive." The psychologist's solution to the problem was to prescribe behavior modification drugs to essentially sedate the children. Their parents would come to Pam and warn her that little Susie had this disorder and that they could not do anything with her. They would relate how they could not control her at home, and how that at school she would be given drugs to retard her hyperactivity.

Pam would work with these children in junior church or in some other children's program and would let little Susie know in no uncertain terms that her word was law, and that she was going to obey, period. There was kindness, a positive incentive to cooperate, and a fun atmosphere about the program, but above all she demanded and taught behavioral discipline. And she got it.

I have watched many of these children over the years. Even though they were a terror at home and diagnosed as hyperactive at school, they would sit up straight, pay attention, behave, and learn the lesson or story in junior church. Their parents would come and ask, "How do you do it?" The answer is relatively simple. Pam teaches discipline and she demands it. Yet the children love her. And the Sunday School bus kids, who for the most part came of their own volition, came back week after week.

In similar fashion, I have witnessed situations where children had been diagnosed as having an attention deficit disorder. Essentially, what child psychologists mean by that is that a child has a very short attention span and has difficulty concentrating on any one thing for even a short amount of time. I cannot speak to the whole spectrum of that matter. But I have watched Pam work with these children who often will absolutely ignore their parents and seriously misbehave in the presence of their parents.

Once she has them, the story is the same. She lets them know through a combination of simple enthusiasm, positive incentives to behave, and old fashioned "I am the boss and you are going to cooperate" that she will not tolerate any monkey business. She insists that they pay attention and commands that attention by using positive reenforcement and dealing immediately with misbehavior.

Curiously, the children who have been diagnosed with an attention deficit disorder at school, very soon become attentive to her program. The parents are amazed. The simple key is the insistence upon discipline and attention. The kids come to her program on Sunday, sit up, listen, behave, and learn. Then they go home and return to being monsters. On Monday they return to being diagnosed as hyperactive or having an attention deficit. The difference is simple. In one program, discipline is instilled and demanded. In the others, it is not.

In short, self-discipline in children must begin with external discipline. Self-discipline is not inborn in our children. It does not come with your child. It is something that must be added to their lives. The parents are the primary agents God intended to instill discipline into their children. Other outside influences may be helpful, but the home in general and the parents in particular are the critical factors.

A Problem by Nature

I have used a little standing joke over the years in preaching on the home and illustrating how our children are born with a sinful nature. I would state, "I did not have to teach our children how to lie," (pause). "Their mother did." This would always elicit laughter from the congregation. Then I would go on to say, "The truth is, my children were born with a sinful nature, and we did not have to teach them how to do what is wrong. They already knew how."

You see, every child born on this earth (with the exception of Jesus Christ) has been born with a sinful nature. This gets to the very crux of the matter. Throughout the New Testament, the old sinful nature we all have inherited from Adam is referred to as the "flesh." Moreover, in the Bible, the flesh is routinely described in terms of lust.

In our 20th-century idiom, we usually interpret that to refer to sexual lust. Though that is *a* meaning of the word, it certainly does not do justice to the broader sense of the word in the Scripture. The Greek word translated "lust" has the broader sense of "desires," or "wants," or "likes." The old nature, the flesh, largely operates on the basis of what it wants, or what it likes, or what it desires. The old nature is not only selfish by nature, it also is "want-" and "self-" oriented. The flesh tends to pursue its own desires.

The Apostle Paul admonished us in Galatians 5:16 to *"Walk in the Spirit, and ye shall not fulfill the lust of the flesh."* Then in Galatians 5:24 he wrote *"And they that are Christ's have crucified the flesh with the affections and lusts."* In a later chapter we will look at the concept in greater detail. However, here it is evident that a major characteristic of our old nature is that of selfish desires, selfish wants, and selfish interests.

Our children are born with a sinful nature that is characterized by self-interest, self-desire, and self-gratification. Later, when they are born again, God creates within them a new nature, but by the time the new nature arrives, the old nature has been around a long time and has in its own corrupt fashion become mature. That old nature will seek what is self-gratifying. It will

...ek the path of least resistance. It will also seek the path of the greatest enjoyment.

As a result, our children by nature are lazy. It is the path of least resistance. It is more self-gratifying to lie around in bed than to get up and get going. (Unless, of course, there is something of greater personal interest to do). Because work or school work does not bring any immediate gratification, the old nature has an aversion to such. "It's boring. Besides it's too much work." Another illustration would be that the old nature is more than willing to drag out toys and entertainments to please one's self and entertain one's self, but by nature, it is not interested in cleaning up the mess afterwards. It is not any fun.

The old nature lives for entertainment of self. It looks for things that are fun. Now fun is not wrong. But when children live for the sake of fun, they are merely gratifying the more basic desires of their old nature. "It's fun to have fun. So let's live for fun."

The problem is that God did not create us primarily to have fun. He created us to serve Him. That means work. He created us to glorify Him. That means being oriented to please Him rather than ourselves. He created us to do what is right. That means placing doing what I ought above doing what I want. Now, do not misunderstand me. I am not preaching against fun. Fun in and of itself is not intrinsically evil, but we have a culture and a generation surrounding us today that has essentially made fun their goal in life.

Children grow from playing with their small toys as toddlers to playing with big and very expensive "toys" as adults. In our modern culture, people earn a living so that they can buy their expensive "toys" and use them in the evenings and on the weekend. For many in our culture today, that is what life is all about because it is the basic nature of the flesh that dictates their lifestyle.

Discipline Directs

Discipline in general and self-discipline in particular force us to do what we ought to do whether it is fun or not. Discipline impels us to do what we ought, whether we feel like it or not. Discipline provides the framework of doing what needs to be done, even though we want to do something else. This has profound ethical, spiritual and moral implications. In short, the more disciplined I am, the easier it will be to do what I ought to do and to be what I ought to be.

Let me give an illustration from my personal life. As a pastor, I am no different from anyone else. Each morning I intend to arise at a certain time. That time will allow me to clean up, shave, dress, eat breakfast, and briefly read the newspaper. It also allows me to spend time in the Word and in prayer.

Each morning I get up in time to clean up and shave. I know about how much time that takes. I *like* eating breakfast and would not think of beginning the day without it. Furthermore, I *like* reading the local newspaper. All of this takes a specified amount of time. Therefore, I know I must arise early enough to accomplish those things.

However I know that I also *ought* to spend time in morning Bible reading and prayer. It is not mandatory. Nobody (humanly) is checking up on me, but I know it is the right thing to do. I know that God has said, *"Study to shew thyself approved unto God"* (II Timothy 2:15). I know His Word has said to *"meditate therein day and night"* (Joshua 1:8).

Now, I am as human as anyone else. I thoroughly enjoy my sleep. As my appointed hour to arise approaches, I would *like* to roll over and sleep some more. More than once the tempting thought has crossed my mind: if I postpone my Bible reading and prayer, I can sleep longer. Therefore, I must make a basic decision. Shall I do what I would *like* to do? Or, shall I do as I *ought* to do? Shall I do what my body *wants* to do? Or, shall I do what is *right?* Notice the difference: doing what I *want* or doing what is *right;* doing what I would *like* or doing as I *ought.*

The difference is discipline. Because I determined earlier that I would seek to do what is *right,* regardless of what I want, my decision is already made for me. I have disciplined myself to do as I *ought* as a matter of principle. It is that discipline I have placed upon myself that enables me to regularly do as I *ought* to do. Self-discipline is the ingredient that causes me to do what is right.

Incidentally, one very helpful key to getting up in the morning is going to bed at night. Isn't that amazing? People come to me and complain that they just *cannot* get up in the morning. They ask how I can get up relatively early each day. My reply is, "Simple. I go to bed at night." I *enjoy* staying up late to read. Occasionally, there is some late-night TV news program I would *like* to watch. But I know that there are important things that I *ought* to do the next morning including getting up in time to be in the Word. Therefore, I go to bed in time to get my necessary sleep and still get up and spend time with the Lord.

Now, that illustration is rather mundane, but the principle begins in childhood and extends throughout life. The devil may see to it that the decision is more profound. For example, one may choose to pursue a personal desire of career choice rather than what he knows God would have him do. Or a teenager may choose to commit fornication because it seems to be fun and exciting, and it seems that everybody else is doing it when he should choose to do right and turn from the temptation.

The principle is the same. It goes right back to childhood. A child must decide if he will duck out of doing homework and go out to play or do as he ought. One thing *fulfills a commitment that ought* to be done, and the other fulfills a *desire* (lust) that he *wants* to do.

If we would go back to the Garden of Eden, we would find Eve making the same kind of decision. She chose to do want she wanted, rather than what she ought to have done. Discipline alone is not all there is to it, but self-discipline can have a profound impact in causing our children to do right.

Beware of the fun philosophy that seems to prevail in our culture. It is anti-spiritual and anti-Christian in character. Children who are brought up to seek fun as a significant goal in life will probably be in for some very hard knocks. Fun is a natural desire of the flesh. Never let it prevail as a matter of course and habit.

What Saith the Scripture?

The Bible has much to say about the principle of discipline. Though the more modern term "discipline" scarcely appears in the English Bible, the principle frequently does. There are a number of Greek or Hebrew words that, though not translated "discipline" in the English Bible, certainly have the concept inherent in their meaning.

For example, the Apostle Paul likened the Christian life to a long distance race in I Corinthians 9. He said, *"And every man that striveth for the mastery is **temperate** in all things."* Those who are in the ministry are admonished to be *temperate* in Titus 1:8. A portion of the fruit of the Spirit mentioned in Galatians 5:23 is *temperance*. Moreover, the Apostle Peter taught that we as God's people are to add *temperance* to our faith. The English word "temperance" essentially means to be self-disciplined. That is, to do what we ought rather than what we want. It is a part of the fruit of the Spirit. It is necessary if we would master the Christian life. It is a necessary quality for spiritual maturity.

In the matter of child training, the Word of God admonishes us as parents to bring up our children in the *nurture* of the LORD (Ephesians 6:4). The word for nurture in the Greek has the sense of discipline as we have thus described it. It has the thought of curbing impulse and desire and subordinating them to what ought to be done. Or in other words, it means *self-discipline.*

Interestingly, the word "disciple" is closely related to the word "discipline." Though all disciples were believers, many believers were not disciples. Among other things, a disciple of Jesus Christ was one who had disciplined himself to follow Jesus Christ altogether.

The words translated *"diligent"* in both the Old and the New Testament come very close to the concept of discipline. It is not precisely the concept of discipline, but it is the product of self-discipline and therefore presupposes it. To be diligent essentially means to be very careful to do what ought to be done.

Proverbs 21:5 says, *"The thoughts of the **diligent** tend only to plenteousness."* Proverbs 22:29 goes on to say, *"Seest thou a man **diligent** in his business? he shall stand before kings; he shall not stand before mean men."* Paul called Titus a *diligent* man in II Corinthians 8:22 and therefore entrusted him with important responsibility. In II Peter 3:14 the Word of God says, *"Wherefore, beloved, seeing that ye look for such things, be **diligent** that ye may be found of him in peace, without spot, and blameless."* Diligence, which derives from a disciplined life, is something the Word of God teaches and is a virtue to instill into our children.

In short, a self-disciplined life will enable us to do what God wants us to do. It also will help us to be what God wants us to be. Though discipline is not necessarily spiritual in and of itself, it provides an avenue through which those genuinely spiritual matters may be developed in our lives. It, therefore, is a major factor in the developing of spiritual character. It is something that should be taught early in life and reenforced throughout the formative years of our children's lives.

True Spirituality

True spirituality is something that comes in considerable measure from faithfulness to the Word of God in our day to day lives. It also results from praying faithfully and actually living in the new nature which was created in us when we were saved. It, in considerable part, comes from faithfulness to the things of God in general and faithfulness to the ministry of the local church in particular. However, the key to being faithful in these things is discipline.

There are many days that I, even as a pastor and spiritual leader, do not *feel* like going to the Word of God nor spending time in prayer, but I must do it anyway. Why? Because it is right! Because God said to do it! Because I ought to!

What keeps me in the Word every single day? A combination of things including schedule, habit, and often a genuine desire for the Word of God. Undergirding it all, though, is a discipline to do what I ought to do because it is right. Perhaps more than anything else, the factor that keeps me in the Word of God day and night is the discipline to just do it because I ought to.

From a pastor's viewpoint, one of the greatest sins of Christian people is unfaithfulness to the Word of God. They know they ought to read God's Word. They know they ought to study it and meditate on it. They believe it. They often love it, and frequently try to practice it. However, when it comes right down to it, I know that many saved people are not in the Word every single day, much less day and night.

There are all kinds of excuses. "I forgot." "I am just too busy." "Something unexpected came up." "There just aren't enough hours in the day." "I had to work overtime." "The kids got sick," etc., etc. As a result, well-meaning Christians are up and down in their Christian lives. Unfortunately, when they are in one of those "downs," Satan often gets the victory.

The one thing that can keep us walking in the Spirit, living a victorious Christian life, and having the joy of our salvation is studying the Word of God every day. In spite of that fact, people do not do it. Do you know the real reason (and not the excuse)? They have not disciplined themselves to do it.

Frequently, the greater reason is that they have not applied discipline to most areas of their lives. Throughout life, they have done things because: everybody else was doing it; it was *easy* to do; or they *wanted* to do it. Many, many people have never led a disciplined life in general, much less in the things of God. As a result they struggle with being spiritual.

Discipline of self will cause one to study the Word every single day. That, more than anything else, will produce spiritual, faithful Christian living. Virtually every time when a person has fallen into sin, gotten themselves in serious trouble, or had major problems in life, and I ask them a simple question. "Have you been faithful in the Word?" The answer is always the same, "No."

The reason they have not been faithful in the Word is that they have never disciplined themselves to do it. The habit of life has been to follow the path of least resistance or whatever the urge or desire happened to be at the time. When we have the privilege of seeing someone get saved who already has discipline in his life, he frequently takes off and begins to grow rapidly as a Christian. He already has a principle of life that will be of immense help to him spiritually after he gets saved.

In like fashion, the key to faithfulness to the things of God, such as church attendance and Christian service, is rooted in the discipline to do as we ought. As a pastor, I have heard just about every excuse in the book of why people are not faithful to the local church. However, once the excuse that is covering the real reason is exposed, the answer is always the same: a lack of discipline to do what they ought to do. *Shallow Christians do* *what they **want** to do. Spiritual Christians do what they **ought** to do.*

This strength of character is taught, in large measure, in the home. Parents, one of the most important principles you will ever teach your children, is that of self-discipline. (Incidentally, the alternative to spiritual living is carnal living. There is no other option.)

Walking in the Spirit

As born-again Christians, we have two natures: the old and the new; the carnal nature and the spiritual nature. That is all there is. We will either live in one or the other. The old nature is corrupt according to its deceitful lusts, but the new man has been created in righteousness and true holiness (Ephesians 4:22-24). At any time, we can be living (or walking) in one or the other of these two natures. Walking in the Spirit (or in the new man) is dependent largely upon the *discipline* of reckoning ourselves to be dead to sin (Romans 6:11).

The strength to walk in the new man again comes from the Word of God and the things of God. Throughout the New Testament, we are taught to crucify our flesh. That is, consider it dead. The Apostle Paul taught that we should reckon ourselves to be dead indeed unto sin. The word "reckon" basically means to make up one's mind. In other words, we need to make up our minds each day to be dead to sin and dead to the old nature.

The key to that decision and determination each day is spiritual *discipline*. This is the determination to do as I ought rather than as I want or feel. This determination stems from spiritual discipline. And it begins early in childhood. Parents, if you would have your children to be spiritual, instill discipline into their lives early. The only other alternative to spiritual living is carnal living. Galatians 5:19-21 paints an ugly picture of that. (If you are not familiar with that portion of Scripture, you might do well to take time to read it.)

We are touching upon the very uniqueness of the human spirit. God has created every one of us as a trichotomy. We have a *body,* (which is obvious). We have a *mind* (which sometimes is not so obvious), and we have a *spirit* (which is totally invisible). The thing that makes me different from my Dalmatian dog is not that she has four feet, and I have only two; or that she has a fur coat and I do not. The thing that is uniquely different between me and my dog is that I have a spirit and she does not. Though I presumably have more intelligence than she does, that is not what makes the human race superior to dogs or other animals. God has created us with a spirit.

What does that have to do with discipline? Simply this. Our spirit ought to discipline our mind which in turn controls our body. If our spirit (particularly that new nature created by God in righteousness and true holiness) controls our mind and thence our total being, then we will not only walk in the spirit, but we will be spiritual. The key factor is whether our spirit controls the rest of our life. When the new nature is the controlling spirit, then we will walk in the spirit. The key is the *spiritual discipline* to do as we ought to do.

Sadly, many a Christian has developed a pattern of life in which they follow the desires (lusts) of their body (flesh) and thereby follow its leading. They accordingly have trouble getting up in the morning because it is easier to stay in bed. They often become overweight because the desires of their body overrule their better judgment to stop eating. A lack of a disciplined life can cause all kinds of trouble.

Discipline Is The Key

Discipline is the key to Christian character. The definition of Christian character we will work with is: *the self-discipline to do what is right.*

I must determine ahead of time that it will make no difference whether doing what is right is easy or hard. I will just do what is right. I must make up my mind that it will make no difference if anyone else is doing what is right. I will go ahead and do it anyway. I must decide that if doing what is right is costly, nevertheless, I will do what it right.

Notice in the preceding paragraph, whether it is fun has nothing to do with it. Whether something is hard has nothing to do with it. Whether something is popular or unpopular is irrelevant. Whether I want to do something or feel like doing something has nothing to do with it. If it is right that settles it; and if it is not right, that likewise settles it. In my opinion, that is Christian character. Parents, we must instill that strength of conviction into our children. Discipline to do what is right is a major principle for training Christian character.

Discipline of the Mind

Discipline is also a major factor in the process of education. Any teacher knows that if a child is not paying attention, he or she is not going to learn. Therefore, behavioral discipline is necessary for education. This is true in Sunday school as well as Monday school. A child who is goofing off is not likely paying attention. Therefore, he or she is not learning whatever is being taught at the moment.

Discipline training of children will help them educationally. Children with disciplined minds will be inclined to pay attention and focus on what they ought to think upon. Undisciplined children will follow their natural desires to goof off, mess around, day dream, and misbehave. Apart from the fact that they may be disruptive to others and cause problems for the teacher, they themselves are not paying attention to what they ought to be focusing upon. Therefore, they get behind in their school work. That shows up in lower grades. They may get discouraged. They may decide that they do not like school. They may decide that they do not like to study and then begin to resist the whole matter.

If a child has grown up making decisions largely based upon that which he *wanted to do,* or what he *liked to do,* or what he *felt like doing,* he is in for a rude awakening. If his life in general has been largely that of seeking fun, school can be a jolt. And for many children it is.

I believe that part of the problem in American schools is the underlying "enjoy yourself" culture. It has reached down through the family to the children. School work often is not fun. Therefore, such children resist it. The overall principle of a disciplined life can make a tremendous change in the educational experience of our children.

I have watched children come into the Christian school at the kindergarten level. Prior to this point in life, the major influence on their lives was their home and parents. As a pastor, I often knew the parents and the character of their family. Children who came from homes in which there was a strong degree of discipline did significantly better in school than did children from homes in which discipline, as a rule, was weak. Discipline and education go hand in hand.

I have listened to many a child whine, "I don't *want* to do my homework, its boring." Or, "I don't *like* school. It's no *fun*." Or, "I don't *feel* like studying." Such children have grown up making their decisions based upon what they like, or what is fun, or what they want to do. Their parents have never trained them in the biblical principle of doing what was right, simply because it was right. Therefore, doing something simply because they ought to do it, is alien to them. The old nature in their lives has become well developed. The principle of discipline could change their lives not only spiritually, but also educationally.

Let us go even deeper into the matter of discipline of the mind. I am convinced that discipline of the mind itself is a major key to learning. Some people struggle with learning throughout their lives because they have never disciplined their minds, much less their bodies. With children, external stimulus is helpful to train their minds to think. As children mature, the human spirit that God has given them ought to take the place of external disciplines placed upon them. If a person is born again, he has the added advantage of having a regenerate spirit to direct his mind.

Genuine studying is work. Learning requires mental concentration which is wearying. There are always things that can distract our minds. To a child, it may be something as simple as staring out the window or occupying his or her mind with the person beside them. It is more fun to tease or make faces at that person than concentrate on the lesson at hand. It is easier to watch something out the window than pay attention to whatever ought to be read or listened to. The point comes right back to discipline. No one has ever taught that child to discipline his or her mind to concentrate.

Parents are guilty on two scores here. First, many a parent errs by encouraging shallow habits of entertainment. Children are allowed and even encouraged to sit and watch TV entertainment. Let us assume that what they watch is not spiritually and morally harmful (though often it is). Yet, they are allowed to essentially place their minds in neutral. They are tacitly encouraged to just sit there and *be* entertained.

(The word "amuse" is made up of the basic word "muse" which means to think and the alpha prefix "a" which means to negate or "not." Therefore, to "amuse" one's self essentially means to not think. And that is exactly what an entire generation of American children are doing.)

Whether it is cartoons, or videos, or other video entertainment, many children are tacitly encouraged to seek to *be* amused. Children are conditioned to be mentally lazy and pursue only what entertains their little minds. When it comes to buckling down and actually concentrating, they just shift gears mentally back into neutral and seek something to entertain themselves again. They are not used to disciplining their minds to do something they do not want to do. Enjoyment and fun for them supersede any sense of doing what they ought.

Secondly, parents are guilty of not taking the initiative and beginning mind training themselves. *The first step is teaching the spiritual principle of doing what is right.* That includes paying attention mentally. Then, parents need to begin basic education themselves. When our children went to kindergarten, they knew all their colors. They knew the letters of the alphabet. They knew basic numbers. They could recognize their name in print. They knew left and right. They knew their address and their telephone number.

Not only had their mother taken the time to teach them these things, she had also done something far more important. She had begun to discipline their little minds. They were learning that even if something was not fun or exciting, they needed to concentrate and learn it anyway. They certainly would rather have played with their toys. Their mother, however, sat them down and began to train their little minds to concentrate on things which may not have been interesting to them, but were things which they ought to learn.

The greater principle was that their little minds were gaining the discipline of concentrating and learning things. They were taught that this was something they *ought* to do. It was *right* to do. Because the principle of righteousness (we always do what is right) had already been instilled, they readily sat down and learned their alphabet, and numbers etc. This was before they ever went to school.

The result was two-fold. First, they had a running start when they got to school. School, accordingly, was not difficult. Therefore, they enjoyed it and formed a positive view of school. Second, and more importantly, they already were well on their way to having a disciplined mind. That ability to discipline their mind when needed, has carried them as honor students right on through their college education. Discipline of the mind is a major key to education.

Emotional Discipline

A disciplined life is a key to emotional stability and strength. We have all witnessed those who under pressure or duress "lose it." They crack and fall apart emotionally. Just as the human spirit that God has created within us has the ability to discipline our mind to do what it ought to do, likewise, our spirit can discipline our emotions to be displayed appropriately.

The word "temper" is commonly misunderstood. For example, we might say that a person has a temper. However, a more accurate statement would be that this person easily *loses* his temper. The English word "temper" is the root of the word "temperance" which means self-control. When a person loses their *temper(ance)* they have in fact lost control of their emotions.

What comes out of one's mouth is what is actually in his heart. Jesus said that it is *"out of the abundance of the heart the mouth speaketh"* (Matthew 12:34). Moreover, the human heart is deceitful and desperately wicked, who can know it. When we lose our temper(ance), what really is in our heart is allowed to come out. That is one reason the Bible is emphatic about controlling our tongue.

In the New Testament, a word is used that is frequently misunderstood. That word is "meekness." Though the word usually is associated with being timid or mild mannered, those are derivative meanings and not the root sense. The associated words in the Greek New Testament translated as "meek" or "meekness" collectively have a basic sense of being even-natured or of controlled emotions.

This will result in one seemingly being mild mannered because he does not overtly react under pressure. In other words, he keeps his cool. He does not lose his temper(ance). The greater thought of "meekness" is of a person who has his or her emotions disciplined. As Ecclesiastes 3 spells out, there is an appropriate time for our various emotions. The basic discipline of righteousness is intended to cause our spirit to restrain our emotions until the appropriate time or place. Hence, Paul taught young Timothy to, *"in meekness,"* instruct *"those that oppose themselves"* (II Timothy 2:25). In short, meekness is the discipline by our spirit to control our emotions.

When people learn to discipline their emotions, they will have built emotional strength. Even as muscles that are often exercised become strong, the frequent control of our emotions by our spirit will lead to emotional strength and hence stability.

Therefore parents, we help our children to develop emotional strength by not allowing them to display emotional outbursts. Emotional outbursts, especially of the negative type such as loss of temper, are not only wrong, but will also lead to a pattern of emotional weakness.

As parents, we must teach our children to control their emotions. In the coming chapter we will give ideas of how this is done on a practical level. Needless to say, parents who will not discipline themselves emotionally will have difficulty training their children to do so. Again, we teach in considerable measure by example and leadership.

The Key to Organization

Discipline is the key to organization. Whatever organizational ability a person possesses comes from the fact that he was taught years ago to live a disciplined life. To be organized requires disciplining the mind to think ahead and to attempt to foresee the needs, problems, and schedule of whatever is being contemplated. *Organization essentially is thinking ahead.*

The reason people are unorganized is that they live in the present, and do not think about what is coming next until it happens. To think ahead means mental work, and it is easier to enjoy the moment than to exercise our minds in trying to think. Mental laziness consigns many to a state of perpetual disorganization.

Unfortunately, many have grown up with the mental habits of taking the path of least resistance. It may be easier and more pleasurable to day dream, or amuse ourselves mentally in any number of ways, or chit chat or whatever. However, until we discipline ourselves to contemplate upcoming needs and plan accordingly, we will never be organized people.

Again, we as parents must teach our children to discipline their minds to do what ought to be done. That means not tolerating sloppiness or carelessness. If we will put responsibility in the context of doing what is right, it becomes much more palatable to a young mind, especially if that mind has already been trained in the principle of always doing what is right.

Likewise, neatness and punctuality derive from developing a disciplined life. We will do our children a great favor by teaching them to be punctual and neat. Neatness is the opposite of being sloppy and disorderly. You might ask your child, "Is it right to

57

be sloppy?" He, as well as you, knows the answer to that. A brief examination of God's creation shows that He did nothing in a sloppy fashion. To straighten up and clean up as soon as is practical is an excellent exercise in training discipline.

Throughout the training of our girls, we always insisted that they keep their rooms clean and neat. They simply were not allowed to be sloppy. And the fact that they had to keep their rooms neat not only helped them to be orderly and organized, but reenforced the principle of doing what is right. It became a discipline in their lives.

Punctuality reflects a disciplined life and the lack thereof shows a lack of personal discipline. It just comes back to the simple matter of doing what is right. When I am not punctual, I am stealing the time of every single person who is waiting on me, and that is not right. Punctuality demands that we discipline ourselves to live by the clock or in some cases the calendar.

Discipline of life dictates that we take the necessary steps to be on time. For example, most everyone knows how long it takes to get from home to work. We know how much time it takes to park, hang up our coat, etc., and get to the appointed place. Organization and punctuality work together to discipline our schedule to get from point A to point B on time. Also, wisdom says to add a little time in case of unforeseen difficulties along the way. A punctual person will therefore discipline himself to allow enough time to get where he ought to be and even plan for unexpected delays.

During my seminary years, I worked for a Christian radio station. As is the case in most radio stations, we lived by the clock. Programming was scheduled not only to the minute, but routinely to the second. If a program was to begin at 9:00 A.M., as the second hand swung up to the twelve on the clock, that program went on the air at the appointed second. It was particularly critical when network programming was involved.

Part of our programming included the live broadcast of the services of the Fourth Baptist Church in Minneapolis. I often worked the Sunday evening shift during those years. The service was scheduled to go on the air at 7:30 P.M. The clock in the main studio and the clock in the church auditorium were synchronized. When the second hand came up to exactly 7:30 P.M., we flipped the switch in the control room. The red light by the auditorium clock went on meaning that the pulpit microphones were live. Those in charge of the service knew that. At the appointed second as the microphones went live, they were ready.

Now such a regimen may seem a little extreme, but it illustrates the point of being punctual. To be late is to be sloppy. It reflects a lack of organization, and it manifests an undisciplined life. Parents, you will help your children to have a disciplined life by insisting that they be punctual.

When I was in sixth grade, I attended a public school in St. Cloud, Minnesota, named Washington School. It was the practice of the school to allow children to walk home for lunch if their parents desired. We all were given exactly one hour for lunch. It never failed that one boy was tardy from his lunch break. The teacher would work on it with him. She tried positive reenforcement and negative reenforcement to correct his chronic tardiness. As far as I can recall, that boy never overcame his lack of punctuality in grade school. It was not only for lunchtime, but for just about anything else.

I have no idea whatever became of him. Later that year we moved to another region of the country. I have known more than one adult, though, who has suffered the loss of a job and jeopardized his career because he would not discipline his time. The pattern or bad habit of being sloppy with schedule inevitably goes back to how a person was trained as a child. I have watched as people who have college degrees and talent in a given area have lost their jobs because they would not discipline themselves to be punctual.

59

Moreover, discipline of one's time can lead to a much calmer life. Someone has said that pressure is running one step behind. Liberty is running a step ahead. When we discipline ourselves to not only be on time, but also a bit early, it removes the pressure and we find life less stressful.

The Key to Productivity

Discipline is the key to productivity in the work place. A disciplined person will accomplish more than one who is undisciplined. Therefore, when it comes time for promotion and advancement, a disciplined person frequently gets the promotion or pay raise, and the undisciplined person gets passed over.

Discipline is the key to financial stability. The number one cause of marital break up is financial problems. The reason people have financial problems usually is rooted in the fact that they are not disciplined in the handling of their money. Space will not allow us to go into the matter of budgets and credit spending. However, people who will not discipline their spending will inevitably have financial woes.

We could continue and expand on much of what has only been briefly touched upon, but the crucial factor in so much of life is discipline. It will help our children spiritually, educationally, emotionally, financially, and productively. It is the key to character. Parents, insist that your children learn to do as they ought to do. In the next chapter we will deal with some practical ideas of how to accomplish that.

Chapter 5 - Back to Basics

The preceding chapter dealt at length with the principle of discipline and its importance. However, we said very little about *how* to actually instill discipline into the lives of our children. This chapter will get into the nitty gritty of doing just that. Ironically, people often want the product of disciplined children, but they get nervous about the process necessary to produce disciplined lives.

Over the years, we have witnessed many parents place their children into our Christian schools. They expressed a desire for their children to have a Christian education and to turn out right. That was the desired product. However, when they found out the rules and policies of the school, they were not so sure they wanted to go through with the matter. They wanted the product, but they did not want the process.

I remember a family who came to our church because they wanted a more disciplined program for their children. However, when they got into that disciplined program, they chafed and bucked. The process of learning discipline is neither a short nor an easy process. That certainly is true in the home. Again, it is the home where the vast majority of self-discipline will be taught.

Discipline begins with the application of external restraints. That is a fancy way to describe rules. Rules tend to restrain our old nature, and the old nature does not like it. Consequently, people often grumble and buck rules, especially children and adolescents. One purpose, however, of discipline is to train ourselves to rise above the desires and whims of the old nature.

In beginning to train discipline into our children, there must be rules. The rules need to be wise. They need to be just. They need to be simple, and they need to be enforced. We will discuss more about that later. You must develop simple rules that govern the life of your children. In our home, especially when our children were small, we had a number of absolute rules. The rules were simple. They were vigorously enforced. Our children knew them clearly. These rules produced discipline in our home.

Three Basic Rules

Let me suggest to you three major, absolute, axiomatic rules for your family. Teach them clearly. Enforce them consistently and vigorously. Do not tolerate any deviation from these basic rules. Each of these rules is based in biblical precept and each goes to the very heart of doing right.

1. We always obey. Few things in family life are more fundamental than teaching children to obey. We positively, absolutely always expected our children to obey when they were given clear instructions. And of course, this relates to the basic biblical injunction of, *"Children obey your parents in the Lord, for this is right"* (Ephesians 6:1). Though the command is directed toward children, parents are to see that the command is obeyed. If children are consistently disobedient, it means that the parents, at some point, have not trained them to be obedient.

Let me illustrate it this way. If my dog is unruly, disobedient, and undisciplined; then who is at fault, the dog or me? Training a dog takes a great deal of time and patience. Training a child takes even more. We positively demanded that our children obey us. If they did not obey, there were immediate and consistent consequences. Every time. Every single time!

Obedience is critically important. Not only is obedience important to maintain order in a child's life, but it also has a profound spiritual implication. One of the most basic obligations that a Christian has is to obey God. The Bible is full of various commandments and principles that we, as His people, are to do.

Furthermore, God has a perfect will for each young person. The basic obligation to God's will is to obey it. However, when children become accustomed to disobeying their parents and getting away with it, they are likely to adopt the same attitude toward doing God's will. If there is a simple key to a victorious Christian life, it is obedience to the Word of God.

Moreover, Romans 6:16 describes how obedience leads unto righteousness. When we obey God, we have done what is right. Obeying God is always right. Therefore, learning the principle of obedience will pave the way for developing the even greater matter of righteousness in our children. Parents, you will do your children a great spiritual favor by insisting on obedience. You are establishing a precedent in their lives for them to obey God as they mature and become independent.

It should be noted that the flesh never is very interested in obeying. We all have heard a child whine, "I don't want to." More rebellious children will defiantly say "NO!!" when their self-will is restrained. Insisting on obedience is a basic way of training a child to subordinate his or her old nature to standards of right.

Later, we will go into considerable detail on the matter of spanking. In our home, when one of the children was directly and overtly disobedient, it was dealt with immediately. There were no ifs, ands, or buts. It was automatic. There was no debate. Obedience was one of the absolute ground rules in our home. We would at times tolerate the plea of, "I forgot." And at times we would issue *one* warning before dealing with negligent disobedience. Flagrant disobedience received no mercy and no further warning. If one of the children was punished for having been disobedient, we always made very sure that she understood her punishment was because she disobeyed.

For example, a basic rule at our house when the children were young was that they did not play in the street. If they violated that rule and were punished because of it, they were reminded that they were being punished not primarily because they played in the street, but because they had disobeyed. Therefore, the basic rule was very simple. Just obey.

When one of the girls became 13 years old, we informed her of a new policy we were implementing. She could not ride in a car driven by another teenager. That may seem very restrictive, but I knew there were many pitfalls of teenagers getting into a car and taking off. She may have honestly forgotten the rule, or she may have conveniently let it slip her mind, but one day she directly disobeyed. When old dad got home and found out about the incident, she was promptly marched to the board room. The board of education was applied to the seat of knowledge, and there was weeping and wailing and gnashing of teeth. After it was all over, we sat and talked as she sniffled and wiped her eyes. I asked her why she had been spanked. She said because she had gone in a car with some other kids. I said, "No, honey, it was because you disobeyed." She knew it. And there was nothing complicated about it. Incidentally, we never again had a problem with that policy. Insist upon obedience.

2. We never lie. The second major rule in our house was that we absolutely would not tolerate lying. If we at this point could take the time and study the character traits of Satan as detailed in the Bible, we would find that more than anything else, he is a liar. Over and over again, the Bible describes him as a deceiver. Jesus said, *"He is a liar and father of it,"* in John 8:44. The Bible says that Satan "beguiled" Eve. That word essentially means to deceive. In Revelation on six different occasions, we are told that Satan is a deceiver.

Now, couple that with the statement, *"The heart is deceitful above all things and desperately wicked . . ."* in Jeremiah 17:9. If we want to keep our children from developing a pattern of life akin to Satan, we must restrain the natural tendency to lie. Furthermore, that old sinful human nature called the flesh, which even the cutest little tyke certainly has, is inherently deceitful. It is naturally inclined to lie, and lying is the very root of all dishonesty.

During our family devotions when the children were little, we frequently would link lying with the more basic principle of righteousness. We would ask, "Is it ever right to lie?" They would dutifully answer, "Noooo." And, "Do we ever lie?" They of course would again solemnly say, "Nooo!!!" "Does God lie?" And they would say, "Nooo!!!" And then, "Does the devil lie?" And they would quickly answer, "Yes!!!" "It's not right to lie, is it?" And they would say, "Nooo!!!" And then we would say, "We never lie, do we?" And they would say "Nooo!!!"

Did our girls ever lie? Yes. They were no different from anyone else. One day when Heidi was a preschooler, my wife came into the room, and Heidi was standing there. She had been told that an item on the table was not to be taken. It had been taken. My wife said to her, "Did you take that?" Without batting an eye, she said, "Patches did it." (Patches was the dog. And Patches by then had become a very well behaved dog. Pam knew that the dog had nothing to do with it.) Little Heidi had directly lied to her mother. Was she spanked? Yes, indeed. But not primarily for taking the item. She was punished because she had overtly lied.

On other occasions one or the other of the girls would blame her sister for some misdeed that was done. When it became clear that she was lying, there would be swift and firm punishment. In the aftermath of the spanking, as she sobbed and sniffled, we would hug her and tell her we loved her. Then again, we would ask her why she had been spanked. Rarely, was it because of whatever the misdeed may have been. She was reminded, it was because she had lied. When asked again why she was spanked, she sobbed, "Because I lied."

Bless their little hearts. The girls soon learned that lying was something that absolutely would not be tolerated. I don't think we ever had an incident with our children lying at school, but they knew very well that if they had it would have been dealt with severely at home. Positively prohibit lying in your children. Needless to say, we as parents had best set a consistent example for them on that score. They will quickly pick up any deviousness and lack of truthfulness in their parents.

3. We always respect our parents. The third and final basic rule in our house was that disrespect, defiance, sassing or any other form of overt rebellion toward us as parents absolutely was not tolerated. Nothing would bring judgment more swiftly than for me to hear our children sassing their mother. They were taught ahead of time that defiance or disrespect was not allowed, period! Should they succumb to the temptation, and on a few occasions they did, they were swiftly reminded of what they had been taught before they were punished.

Again, as we study the Scripture, it is evident that Satan has always been an instigator of rebellion. He inspired the rebellion against God in ages past causing a multitude of angels to become fallen angels. In Jude 8, the Bible says that these, *"despise dominion, and speak evil of dignities."* In modern English, that means they were defiant and spoke disrespectfully of those in authority. Such behavior is Satanic.

Likewise, Satan came to Eve and essentially sought to instill in her a rebellious spirit in the Garden of Eden. I Samuel 15:23 says, *"For rebellion is as the sin of witchcraft . . . ."* It is Satanic in its origins. And rebellion begins with a smart mouth. Needless to say, we did not want that type of attitude and spirit in our children.

Unfortunately, such an attitude already existed. No parents have to teach their children how to sass or to throw tantrums. They already know how.

Let me digress for a moment with an illustration. I was amazed when I took my most recent dog out into the woods for the first time. She was only a four or five month old Dalmatian puppy. Apart from her litter when she was very small, she had never been around other dogs. She had never been out in the woods, but even as a young pup, she instantly and instinctively did what mature dogs do. Though she still had puppy clumsiness, her nose was down, and her tail was up. She ran that distinctive pattern that dogs have of running ahead of their master and checking out the scenery. Yet, she would never get too far ahead. It was as if she had been in the woods for years. How did she know how to act like a mature dog? God created within her those instincts. They were inborn.

Children are born with a rebellious, sassy spirit, and the sooner it is nipped in the bud the better. Our children were no different from any others. They threw tantrums. They attempted to sass and be disrespectful to their parents, but they did not do it long. They quickly learned that it was not tolerated, and they quickly learned that nothing would move Dad to disciplinary action sooner than throwing a tantrum or sassing. They, also, quickly found out that pain and grief from punishment came swiftly. At these times, pain and grief were by no means worth whatever gratification they received from sassing or throwing a tantrum. It just flat was not tolerated, and they learned it quickly.

One of the children would, at times, fight the spanking. She was informed that if she fought and resisted, whatever the original punishment was, it would be doubled. Now, that may seem harsh. However, it did not take too long for it to soak in that rebellion, even during punishment, would not be allowed. We just did not allow disrespect, sassing, rebellion, or defiance at our house. As a result of dealing with it as soon as it raised its ugly head, it had pretty well been purged by the time the girls were of school age.

Our children learned that it was right to be respectful to Mom and Dad. As they grew and matured, that respect remained. Today we have a close-knit, deep love and respect for each other. Do not believe the foolishness that if you deal directly with rebellion, you will only cause a child to be more rebellious. Rebellion and defiance will grow like an ugly, malignant cancer. The earlier it is dealt with, the better.

Now, there were other rules that were applied in our home. The girls were expected to make their beds. They were expected to clean their rooms daily. They were expected to brush their teeth. They were expected to rise relatively early. They were expected to clean their plates. They were not allowed to complain about their food.

As they got older, other day-to-day rules were instigated as needed, but all of these secondary things were subordinate to the three main rules of the house: obedience, honesty, and respect. Those rules were simple. They were clearly explained, and they were immediately enforced. Once those three rules were clearly established, the other things tended to fall into place.

One might think that our home was a rigid, authoritarian, spartan environment. To the contrary, it was a warm, fun, loving place; and one of the things that made it such a sweet place was that there was so little conflict. The things which made for conflict—disobedience, lying, and disrespect, had been pretty well eradicated by the time the girls went to school. Their growing up years are years we all look back upon with a warm glow. Our home has been a little taste of heaven on earth.

Basic Enforcement

There are several principles to be remembered when enforcing rules. First, they must be **immediately enforced**. Procrastination is counter-productive. As a pastor, I have visited in thousands of homes. I have witnessed the following scenario played out numerous times. The details may vary but the basic incident was always similar.

Mom (or, sometimes Dad) would say to Junior, "It's time to go to bed." (Or some other parental directive.) Junior ignored his mother and continued to watch the TV. She continued her conversation with me. After a few moments, she would say, "Junior, I told you to go and get ready for bed." He replied, "Awe, I don't want to." Mom let that go by. A few moments later, Mom became a little hot about the matter. She raised the volume of her voice and said, "I TOLD YOU TO GET READY FOR BED." Junior replied, "But Mom, I WANT to watch my program." Mom tolerated that counter for a few more moments. She then announced, "THIS IS THE LAST TIME I AM GOING TO TELL YOU. GO AND GET READY FOR BED!" Junior, by now himself getting exasperated at being shouted at, shouts back, "I TOLD YOU, I DON'T WANT TO!" Finally, Mom shouts, **"I'M WARNING YOU. MARCH RIGHT NOW, OR I AM GOING TO WHIP YOU!"**

Variations of that scene go on by the thousands every single day in America. The real culprit was not Junior. He knew from considerable experience that Mom could be ignored. Mom was too lazy to get up and deal with the situation. She, in fact, was in her own way contributing to the delinquency of Junior.

Though fighting over going to bed may seem relatively innocuous, a far more ominous pattern was being established. Junior pretty much got his own way and did his own thing. He really was not learning any discipline of life. Moreover, his family life was often filled with inconsistency and friction. Though he may have been a willing accomplice to the crime, his mother was even more guilty for allowing it to go unpunished.

Here is what should have happened in that situation. When Junior ignored his mother, she had two options: (1) Consider that he did not hear her and tell him again. (2) Immediately begin to deal with the situation. If this was a first time offense, it could be handled by a fairly stern warning that bed time is bed time and he was to obey. If this was a repeat offense or if Junior had a bad attitude about the situation, then Mom should march him to the place where she punished her children and deal right then and there with Junior.

If that had been our house, the punishment most likely would have been a spanking. In a coming section, we will look in detail at how a controlled spanking should take place. The point here is that we must deal **immediately** when rules are breached.

One might say, "If I handled the situation described above as recommended, there would be a pitched battle." Well, you had better get on with the battle and win the war while it can still be won. The day is coming when you will not be able to win the battle or the war.

The earlier in life we begin to deal with enforcing the basic rules of the house, the easier the battle will be. Conversely, the later in your child's life that you wait to deal with disobedience and enforcement of rules, the harder it will become.

Secondly, the basic rules of your home must be **consistently enforced**. If it is wrong to do whatever on Monday, you had better deal with it on Tuesday and Wednesday the same way. I have observed so many situations over the years in which a child was disciplined one week for a given offense, but a week or two later that same offense was ignored or dealt with differently. Consistency is a valuable jewel in the crown of parental leadership. Incidentally, inconsistency is a major factor in provoking adolescent rebellion later in life.

Let me illustrate. While in college, I worked as an electronics technician. I learned that every time I touched the contact of a power supply filter capacitor, I received an unpleasant electrical shock. It happened every time. I quickly learned to altogether avoid making such contact. It hurt! Our children need to learn that every single time they violate a household rule, there will be a predictable and unpleasant experience.

Children seem to think that if they whittle away at their parents long enough, the parents will wear down and then give in. Consistently enforce your rules.

When one of our girls was small, she decided one evening that she did not want to stay in her bed. She had been put to bed, but she decided she wanted to get up. She climbed out of her bed and came out into the living room. She was lectured about the fact that it was her bed time and that if she got out of bed again she would be spanked. She was placed back in her bed.

A few minutes later, she came out again. As promised, she was paddled and placed back into her bed. Of course, there was a thundershower, but it subsided. A few minutes later, she came out again. She again was paddled and placed back into her bed amidst rather rebellious crying. (She was throwing a tantrum.) After a while, the thunderstorm went away, and she proceeded to get out of bed and come out again into the living room.

As far as we could tell, there was no legitimate reason for her to get up (such as being afraid of the dark, or having to go to the bathroom, or being sick). She just did not want to stay in bed. So, she got up again. Again, she was spanked. This went on for about half an hour, but she finally got the message: if she openly defied Mom and Dad, she would be spanked. It was consistent. It happened every single time. She finally settled down, sobbing herself to sleep.

That night a major battle was won. Heidi's rebellious little will was broken. She had tried her hardest to challenge parental authority, and she had lost. It was consistent enforcement of family discipline that accomplished that victory. Did we as parents enjoy spanking our little girl? We hated every moment of it. She was our pride and joy. Nothing would have pleased us more than for her to cuddle up to us out in the living room, but we knew how she needed to have discipline developed in her life. After the battle that night, we never again had a serious challenge to the rules of the home. Heidi had learned her lesson, and to this day, she has learned to live a disciplined life.

Finally, family rules need to be **fairly and wisely enforced.** Parents need the wisdom of Solomon. We need to be just and fair in dealing with our children. Though this chapter sounds very authoritarian and unbending, there do come times when children forget, or in their childish immaturity, make mistakes. In our home, we rarely punished our children for breaking something or for spilling their milk or food. Children are immature. With age comes better judgment and coordination.

Direct disobedience, lying, and defiance need to be dealt with immediately and consistently. These are character and spiritual issues. Be very sensitive to the difference between childish foolishness and overt wrong. It is one thing to be long-suffering over an accident or genuine mistake. It is another thing to let disrespect, lying, or direct disobedience slide by.

Positive Reenforcement

The goal in instilling discipline is far more than just producing desired behavior. It is to produce a mental and spiritual pattern of impelling ourselves to do what we ought to do (that is, to do what is right). Desirable behavior is a pleasant fringe benefit. Unfortunately, many a parent views appropriate behavior as the basic goal, when in fact it ought to be secondary. The real goal is to produce a disciplined life. When that happens, not only will the resulting behavior be appropriate in the meantime, but it also will tend to be so on through life.

In seeking to instill discipline of life, let us look at two perspectives. Let us call the first, **positive reenforcement**. That simply means to address the issue positively. The negative will come soon enough, but do not err by forgetting the positive element.

In physics, it is axiomatic that for every negative potential there is an equal and opposite positive potential. If you do not believe that, go out and disconnect one of the cables from your car battery and see if it will start. One side is positive and the other is negative. Both are needed to complete the circuit. Likewise, in the matter of training our children, there needs to be an appropriate balance between the negative (punishment) and the positive (encouragement).

1. Perhaps the greatest positive reenforcement is the matter of love. We will not talk quite as much about this as might be thought, simply because God has created us with an innate tendency to love our children. We do, however, need to work at it. Homes lacking in love turn out children who are spiritually, emotionally, and mentally distorted. History records that Adolf Hitler, Joseph Stalin, and Sadam Hussein came from homes where there was little love.

A home that is all authoritarian and rules likely will produce children who eventually rebel. The mitigating factor is love. Conversely, homes that are all love and little discipline, tend to produce children that go from being brats to delinquents. Never fall victim to the pathetic philosophy that says, "I love my children too much to spank them." If that was not so tragically stupid, it would be funny. Yet, I never cease to be amazed as I run across people who espouse some variation of that philosophy. Tragically, children from such homes inevitably turn out to be disasters. There must be a balance between love and discipline.

Though our home had a disciplined environment, it also was bathed in love. There never was any question in anybody's mind that we all loved each other, and that love remains to this day. We always sought to balance discipline with love. That love was shown verbally, in telling our children, "I love you." It was shown in acts of kindness and in physical embrace. We loved them, and there was never any question in their minds of that.

Again, always balance discipline with love, and much of it. As your children perceive that they are genuinely loved, they will accept discipline. They may not be thrilled with the punishment, but a loving environment will reduce rebelling against the discipline. Always, always, always shower your children with love. Tell them you love them. Show them you love them. Make love as pervasive in your home as the discipline.

God has created us with an innate tendency to love our children. That tendency is perhaps the strongest in the mother. The father, by virtue of the "role" that God has ordained for the man as the head of the home, will tend to be viewed as the authority figure. Therefore, fathers need to work harder at loving their children. For some that may not seem masculine, but it is desperately needed. Dads, make sure that your children realize in no uncertain terms that you love them.

Out in the world, many homes have fathers who, because of the distortion of sin, have never shown much love to their children. Jesus said, *"Because iniquity shall abound, the love of many shall wax cold"* (Matthew 24:12). Sin will refrigerate the ability to love. The sin may be alcohol. It may be immorality or some other variety of sin. The result is that sin freezes out love.

Many children grow up in homes lacking in love. When these children become parents, they often have similar sin in their own lives. Because of the pattern they knew in their own upbringing, they likewise manifest little love to their children. Even after people get saved and begin to grow in the Lord, they tend to do at home as they were brought up. If there was little love in their upbringing, they may refrain from showing much love even now as a Christian. That is all they know.

Christian daddy, even if it was not the pattern of your upbringing, love your children. Tell them you love them. Show them you love them. Make it very clear to them. Then, the more spartan aspects of instilling discipline into their lives are softened by your love.

Before we leave the subject, the matter of love is critical throughout the children's years at home. In fact, it probably is most crucial during their teenage years. The greater principle at hand here is the matter of discipline. However, love in the adolescent years is the ingredient in the family recipe that may mean the difference between rebellion and the intended goal of having them turn out right.

2. Another form of positive reenforcement is to always teach the rules or policies ahead of time. If the children are old enough to understand the reasons or principles behind the rules, seek to explain them. It is far better to sit down ahead of time and talk about a given matter and set forth guidelines (rules). Do not wait until there is a problem, and then react to it. Try to think ahead and stay one step ahead of your children as they develop. Being proactive is better than being reactive. This, of course, presupposes that there is a line of communication between you and your children.

The undergirding concept beneath all of this is the principle of righteousness. Base rules on the principle that it is right. Firmly lay the foundation of, "We always do what's right." Doing what is right then becomes the motivating factor to cooperate. If a rule or policy is related to righteousness on its own merits, then it will be helpful to discuss the matter with the children to point out that it is right.

Teach the principle and rule before a problem crops up. It can then hopefully be reduced to the simpler principle of doing what is right. If the policy is broken, it then becomes a simple matter of dealing with disobedience rather than debating the merits of the rule.

3. Another helpful means of positive reenforcement is the use of incentives to achieve desired behavior. When our girls were small, we used a system of stars on a chart each day they did their daily Bible reading. As they grew older and were assigned household chores, we made another chart and again placed stars on it as they did their respective chores. Once they had a full two weeks or whatever, then we would go out for pizza or some such thing.

When they brought home good school papers, they were proudly displayed. We regularly tried to praise them for doing what was right. They were praised when they cleaned their room well. They were praised when they practiced the piano well.

Whenever the occasion presents itself to praise your children for having done well or having done what is right, praise them. Acknowledge and even reward them for doing what is right. Instilling discipline of life is more than just penalizing when wrong is done. It also is rewarding that which is right. And again, it will be important that there is just as much positive encouragement to do right as there is penalty for doing wrong. Try to think up ways of positively encouraging what is right.

4. Finally, it is absolutely critical that we provide positive reenforcement by example. The old saw of, "Do as I say but not as I do," just will not cut it. An obvious example is of a parent forbidding their children to smoke when they smoke. It just does not work. There are few more powerful teaching tools than that of a consistent positive example.

We will teach discipline of life to our children by being disciplined. We will teach faithfulness to the things of God by being faithful ourselves. We will teach honesty by being completely honest ourselves. We will teach discipline of emotion by disciplining our own emotions. The truth is, to a considerable degree, our children do follow in our footsteps, at least in our basic patterns of life. Lead by example. It will be one of the simplest and most effective things you will ever do.

Negative Reenforcement

Now, let us look at what might be described as **negative reenforcement**. It seems like no one likes to hear about that which is negative. Again remember, for every positive, there is an equal and opposite negative. In the matter of instilling discipline into the lives of our children, that means penalty for doing wrong.

Here is a major principle to remember in applying punishment for wrong doing in our children. **Punishment must always exceed the pleasure or the enjoyment of the wrong doing.** If punishing our children is going to be of much effect, it must be of sufficient degree to deter them from doing it again.

I have watched parents many a time over the years give a swat to a child on their posterior. Frequently the child howled, not because of any pain from the swat, but because he was angry at being challenged in his deed. The swat did not hurt a bit. It is almost comical to watch a child well padded with a thick diaper getting a swat on his rear. It does not hurt in the least. The deterrent in the swat is next to nothing.

Over the years we have had three Dalmatian dogs. In their first year, they were all quite prone to chew things they should not. Two of the three learned a lesson on chewing the hard way, and they learned it quickly. They were sadder but wiser. The lamp cord plugged into the wall outlet was a tempting thing to chew on. And, of course, as their moist mouths eventually made contact with the live conductor in the cord, they learned a lesson they never would forget.

Never again did either of those dogs ever try to chew a lamp cord. The negative reenforcement of the shock cured them of chewing on the cord once and for all. The "punishment" of getting an electrical shock in their mouths far exceeded any pleasure the dogs may have received from chewing on the cord. They never did it again.

When I was a boy, my father purchased a brand new 1955 Packard automobile. It was the first car we had ever owned that had an electric cigarette lighter. I was fascinated with all the knobs on our new car. One day, while checking out all of the new stuff in the car, I pushed in the knob on the cigarette lighter. In a few moments it popped back out. I took it out and examined it. The inner tip was glowing red. So I put the tip of my finger on it. Was that ever a mistake! I dropped that thing and cried in pain. Immediately, a large blister popped up and covered much of the tip of my index finger. For days I had a painful blister on my finger.

The pain of that blister far exceeded any pleasure I might have received from messing around with my father's new car. I never touched that cigarette lighter again. And when it comes to punishing our children, the punishment must always exceed the pleasure or the enjoyment of the wrong doing. To do less is wasted time and effort.

Spanking

That brings us to the matter of spanking. A parent in the church came to me one day and asked, "Pastor, do you believe in spanking?" Well by now, you should know my answer to that.

(Those particular parents had been taught in college that spanking was cruel and violent. Not surprisingly, the child of these parents was grossly undisciplined.)

In the secular, politically-correct world in which we live, the popular view of spanking ranges from it being Neanderthal to child abuse to it being violence to children. Most, if not all, modern child psychologists and pediatric specialists ominously warn against spanking. "Why," they tell us, "it will only cause the children to become violent themselves when they get older.

Furthermore, we do not want to in any way restrict a child's self-expression. "Moreover," they claim, "it may even be a violation of a child's clear constitutional right to privacy."

On a recent national news talk radio program, a high-ranking representative of the United States Department of Justice ominously intoned that all the studies he had read had led him to believe that spanking of children is an act of violence. In his view, it was a factor in the ever-increasing problem of violence in American society.

On another news talk radio program the same subject came up. The talk show host said something to the effect that beating of children is child abuse. Without batting an eye, he equated spanking with beating and child abuse.

People who have been educated in the liberal educational establishments of our society over much of the last generation have been taught that *spanking* equals *beating* and *violence*. However, it does not take a Boston lawyer to realize that those three words are not synonymous. A properly applied spanking is not, by any stretch of the imagination, a beating of a child in the common sense of the word. To try and equate a controlled spanking with violence is just dishonest. The two concepts are scarcely related. Yet, this dishonest propaganda is continually disseminated across our society.

Most pediatricians, social workers, and psychologists really have no concept of proper, controlled, dispassionate application of corporal punishment. In all likelihood, they did not receive such punishment when they were children. Most of which they know about corporal punishment are the horror stories they heard during their formal training. Often genuine child abuse is described as spanking.

In their minds, a spanking is likened to the following scenario: Junior does something that enrages old Dad. Therefore, old Dad, with complete loss of temper, retaliates against Junior and proceeds to beat him half senseless to teach him a lesson.

Sadly, that sort of thing certainly does occur. But that is not the Bible concept of spanking. Yet, that is the stereotype that is repeatedly implied by most opponents of spanking. That type of spanking is without a doubt beating and violence.

However, that is NOT the biblical concept of spanking. As we shall see, the biblical concept of spanking is of a controlled, unemotional, dispassionate application of brief pain to a portion of the body where no lasting injury is inflicted. Moreover, it is effective if properly utilized.

Unfortunately, in many Christian homes the idea is entertained that poor old God is just out of step with the times. He is just an old meany and does not know as much as all these smart experts we have today.

Let me present evidence to the contrary. If the court allows, let me introduce as evidence **Exhibit A**, the state of societal decline in our nation. The endless violence and crime we daily witness all across the land are the result of a generation that was brought up without, among other things, proper spanking.

Biblical Basics Concerning Spanking

A cursory overview of the Bible will reveal that God's Word routinely assumes spanking to be a proper form of instilling discipline into children. Proverbs 19:18 says, *"Chasten thy son*

while there is hope, and let not thy soul spare for his crying."
Here, and in the following portions at which we will look, the
word "chasten" essentially has the sense of what we today call
spanking. Proverbs 22:15 says, *"Foolishness is bound in the
heart of a child; but the rod of correction shall drive it far from
him."* The word "rod" here basically means a branch or a switch.

When I was a little boy, my mother would go out and cut a
switch from the lilac bush growing in the back yard. In fact, as
I got older, she had the audacity to make *me* go out and cut the
switch. That switch was applied to my nearly bare posterior. It
stung. It smarted. It hurt. But I usually got the message.

As I grew older, the diameter of the switch progressively
increased, but it never was enough to do anything more than to
leave a welt on my buttocks. Proverbs 23:13 says, *"Withhold not
correction from the child: for if thou beatest him with the rod, he
shall not die."* Here, the word "beat" does not imply a violent
assault as is the sense in modern English. Rather, it speaks of a
methodical application of a switch to the posterior. Likewise, in
Proverbs 29:15 we read, *"The rod and reproof give wisdom: but
a child left to himself bringeth his mother to shame."*

The clear overview of Scripture is that God has taught us to
spank as a means of dealing with wrong doing, and Hebrews
12:6 makes it clear that the motive is love. *"For whom the Lord
loveth, he chasteneth and scourgeth every son whom he
receiveth."* God deals with His own children because He loves
them. The ultimate goal is to produce the *"peaceable fruit of
righteousness unto them which are exercised thereby"* (Hebrews
12:11). I am not sure of all the reasons for spanking, but some
seem evident. Reasoning and lecturing to children who are not
mentally mature may be an exercise in futility, especially for
small children. They may not understand your lecture. Even if
they do understand, it may not soak in, but they clearly can
understand the sting of a switch on their posterior.

81

It seems that as a child's mental maturity develops, the need for corporal punishment diminishes. Then, verbal and less tangible forms of punishment for wrong become more prudent. But, the Bible clearly teaches spanking as a means of instilling the discipline of righteousness in children. I believe the Bible to be the inspired Word of God. If the Bible teaches that it is wise to spank, then, as a matter of obedience to the Word of God, I will and did spank my children. I happen to believe that God knows more about child training and discipline than the current fads of child psychology.

Practical Basics Concerning Spanking

In disciplining our children, there should be clear policies established ahead of time. The how, what, and for what of discipline in general and spanking in particular should be thought out in advance. Here are some suggestions.

1. Establish ahead of time the basis for spanking your children. Just as you should have predictable rules based on principle, there should be predictable policies to show what will happen when those rules are violated. At our house, it was made clear ahead of time that if our girls violated rules in three particular areas, there would automatically be a spanking. Direct disobedience, lying, or disrespect to a parent brought a swift and predictable spanking.

Moreover, if there was ever any disciplinary action at school, they knew that when they came home, they faced a spanking. They knew it ahead of time. I think that throughout their school years, we may have spanked each girl once for some minor problem at school. If nothing else, the knowledge of retribution at home deterred them from getting into trouble at school.

2. Establish standard implements for administering spankings. We tended to avoid spanking with our hands. The primary reason was that we wanted our hands not to be viewed as instruments for punishment but as always open for help. Though we have often used sticks to spank our dogs when they misbehaved, we at times have used our hands to cuff them if their spanking stick was not handy. However, the dogs then became a little shy of our hands, not knowing exactly if they were going to be petted or cuffed.

Therefore, we have basically used several types of switches and small sticks to punish our children. Probably, the most frequently used implements for spanking at our house were paint stirring paddles. They were easy to obtain when at times switches were not, especially during northern winters. They were of enough substance that they stung when applied but were light enough that they did no bodily injury. (Likewise, I well remember how my father used the back side of a broad plastic hair brush on my posterior when I was 10 years old and older. It had a powerful deterrent effect. All Dad had to do was to threaten to get the hair brush and my behavior was modified.)

3. Establish a standard place to administer spankings. In our home, we generally avoided spanking in the children's respective rooms. We wanted them to view their room as home and a place of "refuge." Therefore, we sought a neutral room in the house. That usually was the bathroom. On the back of the toilet lay the ubiquitous paint stick. When the girls were sternly told to go to the bathroom, they knew what was coming. I suppose every time they used the bathroom for necessary purposes, the stick laying there may have had some useful function of reminding them it was always there, ready to be used.

4. Establish standard spanking policies. Depending upon the age of the children and the nature of the offense, we had guidelines of how many swats they might receive. A standing policy was that if they fought the spanking or were defiant, we would double the amount. It did not take very long before that policy had served its purpose.

As a matter of philosophy, I believe it is very important that spankings be methodical in their procedure. Never, never spank because you are angry with your child. Never let your child perceive that he is being spanked because he made Mom or Dad "mad." If you are angry with him, then wait. It will allow you time to cool off. Never administer corporal punishment in a fit of temper.

Always make sure the children know why they are being spanked. There should be a principled reason such as direct disobedience, or dishonesty, or disrespect. Never should the application of a spanking be vindictive. Never enter into a spanking with the thought in mind, "I'm gonna teach you a lesson, you little brat." It is that sort of thing that raises the specter of child abuse in relation to spanking.

5. Always stay under control. When we spanked in our home, we tried to always be cool, calm, and collected. We tried very much to be dispassionate. That is, we tried to avoid any emotion leaking through. Even if we were upset with the children, we kept that from them. We wanted them to focus on the fact that *they* had done wrong, and because of that there was a penalty. The penalty was sharp, quick, and it soon was over.

6. Spank soon after the offense. We always tried to administer the spanking as soon after the offense had taken place as was practical. Small children especially have a short memory and short attention span. We wanted them to relate the spanking to whatever they had done. We refrained from administering spankings in public places such as grocery stores and the like. Usually in that case, it could wait until we got home.

However, our girls quickly learned that misbehavior at church was dealt with swiftly and unequivocally. When one of the girls was old enough to graduate from the nursery to the evening service, she decided she wanted to continue messing around like she did in the nursery. Her mother tried to hush her. She became mildly defiant, and her mother immediately picked her up and took her out of the service. In one of the back hallways of the church she was spanked on the spot. She quickly learned that it was in her best interest to behave while in the church service. From that time onward she rarely caused a disturbance in a service.

7. Do not reject your children; love them. The aftermath of the spanking experience is an important time. Once our children's rebellious little wills had been dealt with, they would stand there and sob. We purposefully would follow this procedure: after the crying had subsided to sobs, we would take them in our arms and hug them. We would tell them that we loved them and give them a kiss. As they began to settle down, we would ask, "Now honey, why did we spank you?" They might sob something to the effect, "Because I was bad." We would then correct them and ask, "Is that the real reason?" They would nod their head in assent.

Then we would say, "No, honey, it was because you disobeyed" (or lied, or were disrespectful, etc.). We would then talk about it a bit so that it was clear, and they understood exactly why they had been punished. The session of punishment always ended on a note of love. They knew that although Mom or Dad had dealt with them, their parents loved them. Remember always to counter balance disciplinary proceedings with a clear demonstration of love. The two together—discipline mingled freely with love—form a powerful recipe for instilling godly discipline into our children.

Spanking is a means to a much greater end. That end being the instilling of discipline into the lives of our children. It is not the only means, but it is certainly biblical. It is practical and it works. When practiced carefully, dispassionately, in a controlled fashion, and with love, it is an effective means of training our children to do what is right.

Chapter 6 - Separating to Success

We come to what some might consider controversial: the matter of separation from the world. Yet, the Bible is clear on the matter. The idea that separation from the world is a form of legalism abounds in the realm of fundamentalism and even more in the broader realm of evangelical Christianity. The irony of it is that those who view separation as some kind of legalism or right wing strictness frequently lose their children spiritually to the world with which they allowed them to associate.

Legalists in the Bible were those during the first century who sought to add the works of the law to grace as a *means* to salvation. The Apostle Paul addressed this in the Epistle to the Galatians. Adding the works of the law to salvation through grace by faith is legalism. Observing biblical principles of separation from sin and the world is not. The truth is, separation can be a very effective assistance to personal holiness and practical righteousness. Thus, it is of immense value in training our children so that they turn out right.

Steering clear of the world and the things which are in the world is not legalism. It is being obedient to the Word of God which is wise. Obedience or disobedience in this area becomes evident in the teenage years if not before. Many who have fiddled with the world and the things in the world while their children were in their pre-adolescent years were not happy when they began reaping what they had sown.

My father used to use an illustration in his preaching. I do not know if the story is true, but the story clearly illustrated the biblical principle of separation.

It seems that in the old west, a stage coach company was hiring teamsters to drive its stage coaches through a mountainous area. The local office manager had advertised for the position and people began to apply for the job. As they were interviewed, the boss asked each applicant, "How close can you drive the team to the edge of the cliff as you round the mountain." The first fellow replied that he was skilled enough that he could drive the stage coach within three feet of the edge of the cliff. The boss thanked him for his time and called in the next applicant.

In the course of the interview, the boss asked the next man the same question. He replied that he could drive the team and coach within one foot of the edge of the cliff. He likewise was thanked for his time and the next applicant was called in. The boss asked this fellow the same question. He replied, "I would drive the coach as far from the edge of the cliff as I possibly could." He got the job. The story clearly illustrates the biblical principle of separation. There is great wisdom in steering our kids as far from the edge of the world as possible.

You see, the biblical concept of separation is a very positive thing. It will be of great benefit in how our children turn out.

The further we can keep our children from the world and the *things* in the world, the greater the potential they will have to turn out right and have God's blessing upon their lives.

What Saith the Scripture?

Let us first look in some detail at the biblical passages that form the foundation of this principle. Perhaps the most straightforward statement of the principle is found in II Corinthians 6:17-18. The Scripture says, *"Wherefore, come out from among them, and be ye separate, saith the Lord, and touch not the unclean thing; and I will receive you, And will be a Father unto you, and ye shall be my sons and daughters, saith the Lord Almighty."* The clear injunction in its context is to separate ourselves, as God's people, from not only the sins of the world (its **things**), but also from its people (**them**).

The Bible says to come out from among **them** and be separate. This touches upon what the Scripture speaks of as being a "peculiar people" in I Peter 2:9 (also Titus 2:14). We as God's people ought not do what the world does. We ought not go where they go, and we ought not associate with those which the world associates with. We, indeed, are to be a peculiar people.

Sadly, there always have been Christians who have had a yearning for the world and the things in the world. Witness Lot's wife. In that context, remember how Mr. and Mrs. Lot's children turned out. There is a direct correlation between the way Lot and his wife lived and how their children turned out. Genesis 13:12 speaks of Lot pitching his tent *toward* Sodom. There is no indication in the Bible that Lot did the things that the people of Sodom did, but he undoubtedly knew of their manner of life.

The next time we read about Lot, he had moved *into* Sodom. Without a question, Sodom typified the "world" of that day. Maybe it was at the urging of his wife, but nevertheless, Lot did not separate himself from the world of his day. When the day of reckoning came, it was Lot's wife who looked back. She evidently yearned for the things in that world being judged.

Not only did Lot lose his wife to the world, look at how his children turned out. He evidently had at least two married daughters. They chose to stay in Sodom and were destroyed. Two of his other daughters went with him. Later in despair of not having a family of their own, they got their father drunk and committed incest with him.

What an awful mess! *Where do you think they picked up on that sort of thing?* I believe that Lot lost his family when he pitched his tent toward the world.

Let's face it. The world is attractive. It has glamour. It has appeal. It offers fun. It offers opportunity. It portrays itself as being "cool." It offers pleasure and advancement. Many Christian *parents* are seduced by the allure of the world. As Christians they may not go deeply into the world and the gross obvious sin of the world, but they nevertheless think that the world is neat. They are attracted to it and flirt with it.

The closer the Christian family gets to the world, the greater the chances are of the world getting your children. You are playing with fire, and the worst losers will be your children.

You see, the world is the devil's system. It may be defined as the society and culture of the ungodly. Satan certainly is the leader of ungodliness. The Bible calls Satan the prince of this world (John 14:31 and other places). He is called the god of this world in II Corinthians 4:4. In I John 5:19 the Bible says that the whole world lieth in wickedness.

The ungodly world began just outside the gates of the garden of Eden when Cain ignored God and did things his way. It received renewed impetus at the tower of Babel when man again ignored God and tried to reach heaven his own way. The world has been the seed bed of all false religion. It has been the incubator of all wickedness. And as an institution, it is the enemy of God (James 4:4). In fact, in James 4:4, the Bible says that even friendship with the world is enmity with God. James says, *"Whosoever therefore will be a friend of the world is the enemy of God."*

That is why the Bible says in I John 2:15, *"Love not the world, neither the things that are in the world . . . ."* Many Christian parents may *claim* to distance themselves from the world, but they still like to flirt with the *things* that are in the world. The things in the world are the bait that Satan uses to catch your children. Beware!

The Bible is clear. We are not to love the world system and its culture. Neither are we to love the *things* that are in the world. This is where the devil trips up many a Christian family. They are willing to separate themselves from *some* of the things of the world, but not all. In so doing, compromising Christian parents sow the seeds of the spiritual destruction of their own children.

Worldly entertainments will impact your children many times more than you ever thought. When they reach their mid and late adolescence, they may break your heart. Messing around with the *things* that are in the world is like a spiritual narcotic. Those things may be fun and give pleasure. However, that compromise becomes spiritually addictive and destructive. It is very hard to terminate later.

Romans 12:2 says, *"And be not conformed to this world."* One might protest, "But we live in the world." That is right. But you do not have to be a part of it nor be like it. The word "conformed" has the sense of "being molded by" or "of fashioning like unto." In other words, the Bible says not to mold our lives, our minds, our attitudes, our philosophies, our values, or our enjoyments to this world.

It always makes me nervous when I see young people in our church with the latest fad of the world in their dress or hair style. If nothing else, it indicates that they are willingly conforming themselves to the trends of the world in that area of their lives.

91

However, it usually goes much deeper than that. Those clothes or hair styles often indicate an inner love and desire for the world. Sadly, it is often the parents who buy the faddish clothes and encourage, or at least allow, the faddish haircut.

The greater principle here, though, is to avoid patterning our lives after the prevailing winds of the world, and this is far deeper than just clothing or hair styles. It goes to the matter of values and philosophy of life. In fact, it goes directly to the heart spiritually.

Whatever the outward manifestations of worldliness, they are only symptomatic of a far deeper spiritual problem. The individual may not really love the Lord or the things of God (I John 2:15). He has allowed himself to be seduced by the attractions and allure of the world and has turned his heart from God and His will. That is exactly what happened in the Garden of Eden. Therefore, parents, the more of the world you allow into your family, the greater will be the lure of Satan to get a hold of the lives of your children.

Psalm 1:1 says, *"Blessed is the man that walketh not in the counsel of the ungodly, nor standeth in the way of sinners, nor sitteth in the seat of the scornful."* Notice that the Book of Psalms begins with three negatives, and the essence of those negatives is to separate one's self from the world. Incidentally, I know of no greater passage of Scripture dealing with the matter of Christian education than Psalm 1.

There probably is no institution in this country that more embodies the counsel of the ungodly, the way of sinners, and the seat of the scornful than the national public education establishment. With its systemic teaching of evolution which mocks creation, it certainly occupies the seat of the scornful. With its institutionalized sex education (that is little more than sex encouragement), it certainly is in the way of sinners. As it tacitly ignores the things of God under the guise of separation of church and state, it certainly is the counsel of the ungodly. The outcome of Psalm 1:1 is to get our families out of the world and to get the world out of our families.

Moreover throughout the Old Testament, the nation of Israel, as God's people, was commanded to be separate from the heathen (Exodus 33:19, Ezra 6:21, Leviticus 20:24 et al). God knew what was best for His people. I Corinthians 10 teaches us that the things which happened to Israel then are an admonition for us today.

The Goal Is Holiness

Separation is not an end. It is a means to an end, and that end is holiness. I Peter 1:16, among other places says, *"Be ye holy for I am holy."* Holiness, by simple definition, is spiritual and moral purity. It is the absence of sin and impurity. Though we have been made holy in our position in Christ (sanctification), we must also strive to be holy in day-to-day living. Because the world and the things of the world lend themselves to impurity and sin, it is incumbent upon us to separate ourselves and our children from the realm of sin and wickedness, i.e., the world.

There are two basic avenues to holiness in daily living. One might be considered the positive pole of righteousness. As we do what is right, it tends to become holiness. Romans 6:19 speaks of yielding our members (i.e., our bodies) servants to *"right-eousness unto holiness."* As we positively do what is right, it leads to holiness of life.

Conversely, the negative pole of holiness is separating ourselves and our children from sin. Daily separation from the world and the things of the world becomes a practical avenue toward holiness. Because we live with a sinful nature (the flesh), we will never be absolutely holy in this life. Nevertheless, it ought to be the goal of every Christian to be holy.

Paul said in II Corinthians 7:1, *"Having therefore these promises, dearly beloved, let us cleanse ourselves from all filthiness of the flesh and spirit, perfecting holiness in the fear of God."* Notice the object of cleansing ourselves of filthiness is that we might be holy. That is the goal of separation. As we shall directly see, it will have a profound effect upon how our children turn out.

For years, I dutifully accepted the principle of separation in a perfunctory fashion. I knew the Bible taught we were supposed to be holy. Growing up in a fundamental Baptist pastor's home, I knew all of the standard "can't do this and can't do thats, 'cuz they're worldly." However, little by little the Lord opened my eyes to the practicality and love of God in the principle of separation. When I became a parent, I became aware of a whole new spectrum—how practical the principle of separation was in rearing my children. As I read through the Word of God, I began to notice portions of Scripture such as Deuteronomy 4:40 where God instructed His people, *"Thou shalt keep therefore his statutes, and his commandments, which I command thee this day, that it may go well with thee, and with thy children after thee."*

Notice that God said, if we would keep (obey) his commandments, including the matter of holiness and separation, that it would be well with us **and our children**. Wow!! I wanted the best for my children. Here was a specific promise and principle in God's Word that would help my children.

In Deuteronomy 5:29 Jehovah God spoke directly through Moses to Israel. *"O that there were such an heart in them, that they would fear me, and keep all my commandments always, that it might be well with them, and with their children for ever!"* I began to understand that the principles and commandments in God's Word for His people were not just arbitrary "Thou shalt nots." They were for our good and particularly the good of our children.

94

As a pastor, I have preached to our people over the years about obedience to God in separating from the world. It is not only because we are supposed to do it, but because our children will be profoundly influenced by the degree of separation from the world we as parents practice and maintain for our family. It really does make a difference, and the ones to whom the difference will be the greatest are those little ones who call us Mom and Dad. We can make all the excuses we want to try and justify our flirting and messing around with the things in the world, but the harvest will be in our children. Some parents just never seem to get it.

Deuteronomy 12:28 says, *"Observe and hear all these words which I command thee, that it may go well with thee, and with thy children after thee for ever, when thou doest that which is good and right in the sight of the Lord thy God."* We as New Testament Christians are not under the law of Moses. Nevertheless, there is little doubt that the greater principles of obedience and holiness extend to the New Testament church.

Some view the Old Testament law as a restrictive, legalistic, onerous burden, and in some respects it was. Notice that on three different occasions, God said that if His people would carefully obey, it would not only be well with them, but also with their children. The truth is, there is great wisdom and mercy in the law itself. Though portions of it may have been burdensome, overall it was a great blessing, particularly for the children.

Today, New Testament Christians are not under the law. We never were because it was a covenant made with the nation of Israel. In any event, the law has been fulfilled in Jesus Christ. This point remains, however. If we as the people of God will be careful and diligent in obeying His Word, especially in the matter of personal separation and personal holiness, it will be well with our children.

Years ago, I determined that I would pursue anything that God said would be good for my children. The principle of separation is not legalistic. It forms the basis for magnifying the blessing of God upon our children.

Spiritually Sour

Thus far in this chapter we have discussed the matter of separation largely as a principle and as a matter of Bible doctrine. Let us move on and begin to look at the practical outworking of this principle.

Let us stop and think for a moment about milk. It is seemingly pure and wholesome. If it is properly refrigerated, it will last for quite some time. However, within the milk itself is bacteria. If the milk is not pasteurized and then refrigerated, the bacteria from within the milk will begin to grow and before long the milk will become sour. Sour milk is not a pleasant thing, much less of any great value.

Likewise, think about a little girl. Her open countenance and innocence are seemingly pure and wholesome. However, allow the bacteria of the world and its philosophy to begin to work in that sweet child. Before long, that little girl may become a spiritually sour, rebellious young woman.

We have all seen it. In their preschool and elementary school years, they were so cute, so innocent, so wholesome. However, when they reached their adolescent years, they became rebellious, sour, and sometimes incorrigible. That innocent, open countenance became hard and defiant. Their clothing and hair styles became the uniform of whatever the latest fad of rebellion was. Plus, they may actually be doing the stuff that they look like. What happened?

You might say, "Well that's just the way it is. That's human nature. All kids do things like that. In every generation it's the same." Well, I am sorry. Not all kids do that sort of thing, and not all kids go sour and become rebellious spiritually.

I remember one young lady, who in her elementary years was the picture of innocence. Her homeliness was almost cute. She was a little shy. She never seemed to cause any trouble at church or in our Christian school. She did well academically and came from a home of faithful, sacrificial Christian parents.

However, by the time she was mid-way through high school she had become hardened not only in her heart, but certainly in her countenance. She began to dress provocatively. She openly fought with her parents and became grossly promiscuous. Before she was 21 she had several illegitimate children. What happened?

I think of another family in our church. It was the days before our Christian school, but they were faithful to all the ministries of the church. The children were cute, wholesome, and all-American looking, and as they became teenagers, they were faithful to the church youth group. Yet, as they grew into their mid and later teens, the bitter fruit of sin and unlawfulness manifested itself. The one daughter who was so pretty and sweet became hardened in her countenance and became known in the community for her promiscuity. Her brothers, one by one, were arrested for various offenses. What happened?

I think of another fellow whose dad was a deacon in our church. Both of his parents were very active and faithful in the church. They had been strong promoters and supporters of the Christian school. This little guy was the picture of innocence. He was a stereotype of a little boy in Sunday School from a devout Midwestern family. Yet before he had graduated from high school, he had been expelled from the Christian school for several things including: drinking, drugs, and playing publicly in a rock band. How could this happen?

I am mindful of a dear Christian family who sacrificed to place their children into the Christian school. They were faithful and loyal. There literally "never was heard a discouraging word" from their lips. Yet, when their sweet, pretty, shy, seemingly innocent little girl got into her high school years, she was expelled from

tian school for sleeping with her boy friend.
n, she promptly moved in with him and continued her
fornication. How could this be?

The list goes on and on. I think of one young lady who was a
pastor's daughter in another church. She seemed the epitome of
a decent, wholesome, modest, discreet, spiritual girl. I encouraged
my daughters to try and get to know her when they went to
camp. I thought that this was the kind of girl I would like to set
forth as a role model for my daughters.

However, when this girl got to Bible college, she was expelled
for fornication. She also moved in with her boyfriend who
likewise had been expelled. The upshot of this sad episode was
that her father left the ministry. What a tragedy! But how could
that happen?

He had been a deacon for years. His son was in the Christian
school and was faithful to all of the services, at least outwardly.
The boy went to camp every year, vacation Bible school every
year, and all the youth activities as he got older. Nevertheless, by
the time he was out of high school his repertoire of activities
included X-rated pornographic video viewing, drinking, fornication, smoking pot, and general rebellion. As soon as he could
leave home, he faded from the church. Why?

Sadly, after 25 years in the ministry, I could continue to fill
page after page with similar stories of young people who have
either been a part of our church or have been in neighboring
churches. In my opinion, there was a common strand in every
one of these tragic situations. Though I surely did not know all
of the ingredients of their personal lives, one thing either was
obvious or became known later. At one point or another, there
had been a compromise of the principle of separation from the
world in the personal lives of these young people.

In some cases it was by their parent's example, tacit approval,
and acquiescence. In other cases, the children secretly and
surreptitiously began to dabble with the things of the world. The

spiritual bacteria of the world found a welcome reception in the own carnal natures. Between the two, these young people were drawn into sin and the world. The world soured them spiritually.

You may have spent thousands of dollars in Christian education so that your children turn out right. At the same time you may neutralize, if not negate, the influence of the Christian school if you allow the world and the things of the world through the back door of your home.

What are some of the *things* of the world that Satan will use to snare your children? Let us look at some of them. Remember, this is not a discourse on legalism, but a lesson on helping your children. The more you can get the world and the things of the world out of the sphere of influence on your children, the better it will be for them.

The Power of Music

I am about to take aim at a sacred cow in the lives of many a Christian family. I am targeting dead center the matter of their music. One of the most powerful spiritual forces in life is music. It is universal. People may be totally ignorant of the spoken language of a given nation, but they can readily understand the music of that nation.

Take for example the classical music of Sibelius, who was Finnish. Though my wife is part Finnish, I do not understand a single word of Finnish, but I certainly am moved and stirred by the music of Sibelius. I understand clearly the language of his music, and its appeal is universal regardless of language.

Likewise, when the Beatles swept the world in the mid 1960's, in many countries their lyrics were not translated, and they sang in an "unknown" tongue. Yet, the influence of their music was virtually the same as in the English-speaking world. The basic language of the music is universal. Now, whether you *like* the

...us or the Beatles is beside the point. You can ... the underlying musical message. Sibelius was ... Beatles were rock 'n roll.

...we go much further in the matter of music, it will be helpful to discuss a little about music in general. From a Christian point of view there are three kinds of music.

One is **sacred music.** Sacred music is that which is distinctly Christian. It honors the Lord and glorifies Him. It has no taint of the world's "sound" or style. It is godly music.

Then there is **secular music.** Secular music is just as its name implies. It is not sacred, but it really is not of the genre of the world spiritually. Secular music might include such selections as the "Stars and Stripes Forever," "Happy Birthday", "The Michigan Fight Song," or much classical music.

Then there is the **world's music.** The world's music is that which characterizes the society of the ungodly. We might be less euphemistic and call it the devil's music which may sound strong, but is true.

Entire books have been written dealing with the world's music and its destructive influence spiritually. However, let me give just a few selected examples of songs and song titles that illustrate my point. About 25 years ago, a song entitled, "Strangers in the Night" was popular. As the song unfolded, the lyrics told of how two strangers in the night would be "making love before the night was through." It does not take a rocket scientist to figure out what that was alluding to. Then, another group came along with an even more explicit title called, "Let's Spend the Night Together." Much of the world's music over the past 30 years has focused on such base themes as adultery, fornication (i.e., sex euphemistically referred to as love), rebellion, and even drug usage.

This book is not to document and detail the current trends of the world's music. However, shelves full of books have been written on the subject over the past generation. The world's music has been the antithesis of anything godly or pure. It is a powerful influence spiritually and the devil knows it.

Multitudes of Christian young people have been enticed into the world simply through listening to the world's music. It is attractive to the ear. It can be fun to listen to. It is habit forming, and it absolutely will influence spiritually. You show me the music you allow in your home and I will tell you how your children will turn out spiritually. It is that critical.

Perhaps, you have noticed that thus far I have basically avoided using specific terms such as rock 'n roll, or country western, or the blues, etc. Of course, there are all kinds of subsets within any of these broader categories. Here is why I have thus far avoided naming specific categories of music. People will be critical of, for example, rock 'n roll, but they will listen to country western. Sometimes they will be critical of both, but listen to the big bands of the 40's and 50's. Perhaps they will listen to the pop music of the 50's and early 60's.

What they fail to understand is the greater principle. It *all* is the music of the world. To be sure rock 'n roll, particularly in its more gross forms, is obviously of the world. In fact, it is from the pit of hell, but the music of the 40's and the big bands is just as much of the world. God's people back then preached against it.

For example, Glen Miller's notable song "In the Mood," was suggestive of being in the mood for you know what. That is not as explicit as some of the more recent filth, but it is still in the same category. Guys like Elvis Presley were considered lewd in their day, and though contemporary rock performers gross him out by comparison, they still are all of the world. Need I point out the corrupt and (to put it mildly) the sinful life styles of the world's musicians? Elvis lived a debauched life, and his successors have only gotten worse.

So many Christian parents get into the silly game of categorizing some of the world's music as not as bad as such and such. They use euphemisms such as "light" rock or "golden oldies." It is still the music of the world. It is going to be virtually impossible to forbid your children to listen to the world's music of *their* day when you as parents continue to listen to the world's music of *your* day. The world's music will hook your children into the world just as surely as drugs or booze.

You will recall the stories listed earlier in this chapter and elsewhere in this book of young people who slid into the world. Do you know the common denominator in virtually every one of those situations? They were into the world's music.

Later in the book, we will go into some detail concerning the flesh and the spirit. The flesh once again is the old nature through which all sin enters the Christian life. I know of few things that will slip a Christian into the old nature more quickly than the world's music. As a Christian continues in the old nature, inevitably he or she will, at the least, be tempted with the lusts of the flesh. They very well may succumb to those temptations.

You show me Christian young people who, despite determined efforts by their parents to the contrary, wind up in the world. If I were a betting man, I would lay money on the fact that those teenagers had been into the world's music for a long time.

I recall counselling with a fine man in the church. He was heart broken over the rebellion and deep sin his teenager was getting into. Then he admitted he had given in and allowed that teenager to listen to rock music hoping maybe he would cooperate on other things. That probably was the worst thing he could have done. That young person proceeded to go about as deep into the world as can be imagined.

As a teenager, I became hooked on rock. It was only by the grace of God that I did not go further into the world than I did. One thing was certain: my heart was there. I know that it was the music I listened to 30 and 35 years ago that helped the world to get a hold on my life.

I love my parents dearly, and I believe that they instilled into me a godly heritage. (Though at the time, I did not appreciate it.) However, if they made one mistake in my upbringing, it was that they allowed me to have a radio in my room. A radio is a piece of electronic equipment which is not intrinsically evil, but it was through that radio at my bedside that I became acquainted with the world's music. I developed a desire for it, and it profoundly influenced me for the worse in my teenage years. That radio introduced me to the world. I would sit in my room or lie on my bed and listen to the top forty day after day and hour after hour. That, perhaps more than anything else, drew me into the world before I was saved.

I am not exactly sure how it works, but young people seem to have an innate "radar" to find the world's music on a radio. And they do. For that reason we did not allow our girls to have a radio in their room. We just did not want to place the temptation before them. To this day they have never gained a taste or appetite for the world's music. I think that is a significant factor in how they have turned out.

Likewise, we did not allow them to have their own stereo or tape recorder in their room until they were seniors in high school. By then, they had already formed firm convictions about music and righteousness. We had radios and stereos in other parts of the house and they were used regularly. Everybody knew exactly what kind of music that would be played . . . either sacred, or perhaps, classical.

I am not saying it is wrong to allow your children to have a radio or stereo in their room, but I am saying that you are putting a **big** temptation into their hands. We figured we were not going to take any chances and allow the devil to unduly tempt our children. They formed their convictions and standards about music, and *then* we allowed them to have radios and stereos.

Our girls were too important to us and we loved them too much to allow the devil to sneak into their lives through the world's music. Sadly, he has done so in the lives of untold multitudes of young people in Christian homes.

Just remember these simple paraphrases, "Come out from among them and be ye separate and **listen not to the unclean thing**." Or, "Love not the world, neither the music that is in the world." Or, "Blessed is the man who listens not to the counsel of the ungodly musician."

Let us go a step further. The collective genre of music known as CCM (Contemporary Christian Music) is a synthesis of the world's music and sacred music. Or put another way, it is a compromise between the world's music and sacred music. Unfortunately, there is more of the world than godliness in most CCM.

In a given selection of music, particularly a vocal selection, there are at least five constituent parts. (1) There is the melodic line. (2) There are the lyrics (words). (3) There is the chordal structure. (4) There is the rhythmic structure. Lastly, (5) there is the style of the performer(s).

In most CCM there is (1) a very distinct and often heavy conformity of the performing style of the musician to the style of the world. (2) There is almost always a conformity to the world's characteristic rhythmic structure, i.e., a rock beat of one degree or another. (3) There usually is a conformity to the world's style of chord structuring. (4) Frequently, the style of the melodic line parallels the style of certain types of the world's music. (5) Finally, there are added Christian lyrics (and often they are shallow and without basis of Scripture).

Now then, we have a kind of music that has four of its five constituent parts conformed to the world. Pay very close attention to the overall sound of CCM. It usually is very little different from the music that is heard in the world.

Time and space do not allow me to go into the greater issues of compromise and the justification for such music that CCM proponents attempt. And you might ask, "Well, what's this have to do with raising my kids to turn out right?" Well, believe it or not, there is a correlation between CCM and how your young people are going to develop spiritually.

First, CCM is, more often than not, shallow spiritually in its message. Secondly, being a synthesis between the world's music and sacred music, it is a compromise of principle. Thirdly, on a practical level, it will absolutely influence your children. It is a kissing cousin to the world's music. When young people become accustomed to and attracted by the "sound" of CCM, it is a very small lateral "cross over" into the world's music.

I remember a Christian college that had requested to come and present its program in our church. Because I knew the president and viewed that college favorably, we invited them to come. While most of the group was in their van in our church parking lot waiting for the rest of their group, I pulled into the parking lot. The day was cool so their van had most of its windows rolled up. Nevertheless, I could clearly hear the booom da booom da booom of the van's stereo blasting out some sort of music.

I couldn't distinguish any words through the closed vehicle, just the loud booms and thuds of the rock rhythm on the tape they were playing. They told me they were playing "Christian" music. However, from any distance no one could tell the difference between their stereo and that of some rock 'n roller booming down the street.

The point I am making is, the "sound" of much CCM is virtually identical to the sound of the world's music. It is a very small step for Christian young people to "cross over" into the world's music altogether. Then, we are back to square one mentioned earlier in this section . . . the world's music.

Now you may think, "Give me a break, preacher. You just don't like that stuff, so you are critical of it." Well, let's get back to the basic proposition of this book. Train your children so they turn out right. Believe me, this is a critical factor in their lives.

Let me tell you several stories. I am mindful of a pastor who allowed and even tacitly encouraged CCM in his church. When I would visit in his office, there usually was the local Christian radio station with its CCM playing in the background.

His teenage son was into CCM in a big way. He really "dug it." And why not? From time to time it was in the pulpit of his father's church. It was on the radio around home and in dad's car. However, this boy, by the time he had gotten out of high school, had managed to steal the virginity from a number of girls in the church youth group. He was dabbling in booze and drugs.

He became such an embarrassment to his father and his ministry, his dad finally had to resign the church and go elsewhere. Though you may disagree, I remain convinced that this fellow's slide into the world was influenced by his music. The CCM he liked helped him to "cross over" into straight rock. The world's music did its thing on him. He was a terrible testimony in his own right. Not only did he drag others into sin, but he also almost forced his father out of the ministry. I blame it on their music.

I think of another preacher in a different state. He was a good man. He preached the Book straight. He had a good philosophy of the ministry. His church was a going church. But alas, he too not only allowed CCM in his pulpit, he aggressively promoted it. Special music in his church wasn't much different from going to the Grand Ole Opry in Nashville.

However, this pastor couldn't figure out why his own children were drifting into the world as well as the young people in his church. I know why. It was the music he thought was so neat. Here is the irony of it. It helped boost his church attendance. However, in so doing, he was sowing the seeds of the moral and spiritual destruction of his own children. That man today is a saddened, disillusioned pastor.

When we began the Northstar Baptist Church in 1989, we met for the first two years in a rented chapel in a private high school.

I'll never forget one summer Sunday evening. The school administration had informed us ("warned" might be a better word) that there was going to be a Christian (rock) concert elsewhere in the building that evening.

We used the small chapel. The rock concert promoters rented the big, one-thousand-seat auditorium down the corridor. Several Christian rock groups arrived that morning and began to set up. I stood in the shadows backstage unnoticed and watched them. Of course, they looked like any secular rock group. Then, to my amazement, I watched as one of the male members of a group proceeded to lewdly fondle and sexually touch one of the girl volunteers from a local church helping him. It was brazen and disgusting. She willingly allowed it.

That evening, the concert fired up. The large building reverberated with numbing decibels as the Contemporary Christian Concert blasted away down the corridor. We watched as police were necessary to control the crowd. There was the standard punk-rock look complete with dyed and spiked hair, ragged to the point of being immodest clothing and all the other accoutrements of a rock concert.

During the intermission, the crowds poured out into the corridors and onto the lawn. The air was thick with smoke. There was necking and crude epithets shouted. Now mind you, this was a Christian concert because the music was genuine, authentic Contemporary Christian Music.

I wondered how many Christian parents had any idea of the atmosphere of that "Christian" concert they allowed their young people to attend. All in all, it wasn't much different from a secular rock concert. Perhaps, the only difference was that booze and drugs were not openly flowing.

The Bible says, *"Be not conformed to this world."* And that principle has a very practical reason. When we conform ourselves to the world, it is not long before we are doing the same stuff that the world does. Contemporary Christian Music, with its

107

many different nuances, is compromise with and conformity to the world. It will adversely affect your children spiritually and how they turn out.

The principle of separation from the world absolutely means separating from the world's music. Later in this chapter, we will get into other areas of separation such as TV and Hollywood. However, let me just say this. The matter of the world's music will have a more profoundly negative effect on your children than raunchy TV. Music is spiritual. It reaches into the soul, and it is powerful. The devil knows it. Sadly, many Christians are willingly naive about its influence and power.

The Tragedy of Television

However, there is much more to the world than just its music. Another area that is insidious spiritually is the majority of stuff on the television. For the most part, it is of the world.

I was shocked one year when a teenage girl in our church informed me that she was looking forward to summer vacation so she could watch all the soap operas. And she was so innocent in telling me that.

I own several television sets, but believe me, we have **controlled** what has been shown on the TV in our home. Do you recall the incident found in both II Kings 20 and Isaiah 39 where Isaiah the prophet said to King Hezekiah, *"What have they seen in thy house?"* The context there is of Babylonian emissaries who were spying. Nevertheless, there is an application for today of what comes into our home through the electronic media.

As a rule our TV set was off more than it was on as far as our children were concerned. Our children did not even know that there were cartoons on Saturday mornings until they were in about first grade. They went to school and heard their friends talking about them. We still didn't turn on Saturday morning cartoons.

We had a basic rule in our house. The children couldn't just go and turn the TV on. They had to ask permission to watch a specific program. If Mom and Dad did not think it was wise or good for them, the set did not even go on.

We had another standing policy at our house. We did not watch any of the so-called prime time major network programming. We did not allow our girls to watch the sitcoms or the police shows or the romance stuff. It was forbidden. By just watching the "promos" of those programs on the evening news, it doesn't take much discernment to know how raunchy and of the world that type of programming is.

We have never allowed our girls to go to the movie theater. As far as I know, they have never been inside one in their lives. Therefore, we rarely allowed them to watch "Monday Night at the Movies" or the "Tuesday Night at the Movies." We did not want the world to come into our home via the television set. Moreover, we wanted our girls to learn to entertain themselves in better ways both intellectually and spiritually.

They were encouraged to read. They were encouraged to develop their music. They were expected to do their school work before anything of an entertainment nature was allowed, and they did. So what did our girls watch on TV over the years? The little they did watch usually amounted to things like reruns of "Leave it to Beaver," or "Mr. Ed," or "Andy Griffith." We allowed them to watch things like "The Sound of Music" or "The Wizard of Oz." For the most part, TV was not a major part of the lives of our children.

Parents, you will be well served (not to mention your children), if you keep the TV to an absolute minimum in your home. Control it. It certainly is a matter of separation from the world. TV is not intrinsically evil. As a rule, however, the less

TV your children watch, the better they will be, both spiritually and educationally.

One thing that concerns me as a pastor is the invasion of the rented videos into Christian homes. A VCR is not intrinsically wrong. And watching a video at home is not evil. But the majority of commercial videos are straight from Hollywood. There probably is not a stronger bastion of the world than Hollywood.

Forty and fifty years ago, fundamental Bible-believing people knew that Hollywood was wrong. It was universally preached against from the pulpit of any fundamental Bible-believing church. Hollywood has only become worse in the last forty or fifty years, but now Christian people go out and rent Hollywood and bring it into their homes on a wholesale basis. As I recall, my Bible said, *"Come out from among them, and be ye separate, saith the Lord, and touch not the unclean thing"* (II Corinthians 6:17). And *"Love not the world, neither the things that are in the world"* (I John 2:15).

No dedicated, God-fearing Christian parents would allow a harlot to come into their home and display herself in front of their children. They would much less let them see a bedroom scene with such a woman. Yet it happens all the time on the TV.

No godly parent would allow some character to come into your home, smoking, cursing, drinking, mocking things you hold sacred, and then acting out violence in front of your children. But it happens every day on TV and rented video cassettes. Ironically, Christian parents are allowing the world to come into their home through VCR's and TV sets.

Mom and Dad, I guarantee that the major losers in your home will be your children as a result of viewing TV and rented videos. They will dull your children spiritually and present the world to them as glamorous and attractive. They seek to draw them into the world altogether.

You may pooh pooh this warning and think I am old-fashioned and narrow. The sad and tragic true stories presented throughout this book of many children from Christian families show that when you mess around with the world, you will have consequences. Those consequences will show up in your children. That is serious business!

Trends That Tell

As our children were growing up, we did not allow them to follow the fads and trends in clothing and hair styles. You say, "Why?" Because the Bible said, *"Be not conformed to this world"* (Romans 12:2). There are probably few things that are more conforming to the world for an adolescent or pre-adolescent than being in step with the current dress or hair fad.

We did not allow it. We wanted our girls to know that they were a peculiar people. They were different from the world. We did not want them to feel at home with the world's crowd. When the girls out in the world were running around in shorts or tight blue jeans, our girls wore skirts or culottes. You protest, they *must* have been peculiar. Isn't that what Paul said in Titus 2:14 when he spoke of Jesus Christ purifying unto Himself a peculiar people?

We just did not allow our girls to wear immodest clothing even when they were little. Though modesty of dress may not be a big deal for elementary school children, we did not want to establish precedents we would have to wrestle with later. Our little girls never ran around in shorts.

When they became attractive young women, it was no struggle to straighten out that kind of problem. They already were long accustomed to dressing modestly. I Timothy 2:9 instructs us that godly women are to adorn themselves in modest apparel. That word "modest" in the Greek New Testament literally means a

111

lengthened garment according to Thayer's Greek lexicon. That pretty well precludes short skirts or short pants.

Now, before you consign me to being some kind of ultra, right-wing nut, let me tell you a few stories of events I have witnessed over the years. When I was an assistant pastor in the early 1970's, the fad of the day was the mini skirt for teenage girls. In fact, the micro-minis were in.

As a young and inexperienced assistant pastor, I may not have handled the matter as wisely as someone older and more seasoned. However, here is what I did. I ordered a quantity of the little booklet written by Evangelist Hugh Pyle entitled, "Skimpy Skirts and Hippy Hair." In one of our youth meetings, I distributed the booklets to each of our teenagers in the youth group. I then asked them to take it home and read it. It dealt with both sexes and their conformity to the prevailing fads in the world at the time.

Well, one 14-year-old girl, who was notorious for wearing skirts about as short as can be imagined, took the booklet home and showed it to her parents. That same week I was helping the men in the church spray paint one of the buses of the church. I came home from the church bus garage for supper that evening covered from head to foot with over-spray of paint. The telephone rang. It was this girl's dad. He was livid and demanded to see me right now! I told him I was a mess and had paint all over me. No matter. He wanted to see me, NOW!

So, I went to his house which was just a few blocks away. He raged, "How dare you give such a booklet to my daughter. What kind of filthy mind do you have, anyway?" He and his wife took turns ripping me up one side and down the other. Well, the girl remained in the youth group and wore a little more modest clothes at least to church youth functions. However, she still wore the micro-minis to school and around town.

Tragically, by the time she was 16, she was pregnant. Just as sad, her older sister, who dressed the same way, wound up having two illegitimate children before she was 19. And these girls came from a rather well-to-do suburban family living in a lovely new, suburban home.

Consider what the result might have been had this family practiced the principle of separation concerning modesty of dress. Their daughters may have had a different conclusion. I think so.

I think of another girl in our church. Her dad was even a deacon, but as a seven- and eight-year-old, her mother would dress her in short shorts and a bikini top in the summer. Now shorts and a bikini top may not be a big deal on a seven-year-old girl. But when that girl got to be 17 and wanted to run around dressed the same way, there was a real battle in that home. Her parents had foolishly allowed a precedent of dressing as the world dressed. And the girl liked being accepted by the in-crowd in the way she dressed.

When she became a teenager, she gave her parents fits. She had fallen in love with the world. She wanted to dress like the world. She wanted to live like the world, and be like the world. Separation in general was weak in that home. That no doubt was why separation from the world in manner of dress was so easily compromised. Those parents would have saved themselves and their daughter much grief by being consistent in the matter of separation from the world and the things of the world.

I have always been nervous when the boys of our church followed the current fad of hair styles. A given hair style may not in and of itself be evil. However, when young people are allowed or encouraged to follow each wind of fashion in the world, I am afraid they are tacitly conforming themselves to the world (at least in their appearance).

Our young people don't have to look like "nerds" or "geeks". We can dress and groom them properly and attractively without following whatever the latest fad or style is. What is ominous about so many of the fads of dress and hair style is that they more often than not are a parroting of the way rock stars deport themselves.

Those of you old enough to remember the Elvis era will remember the fad was the duck tail hair style like Elvis wore. Then the Beatles came along and the in-thing became the mop-top look like the Beatles had in their early days. Then as the rock set rebelled against the Viet Nam war, the hair style became the hippy hair look. Dutifully millions of American teenage boys promptly began to grow their hair like whoever their hippy rock hero was.

Sadly, a lot of Christian young people did exactly the same thing. They were conforming themselves to the current fad of the world in their hair style. They also tended to pattern themselves after the lifestyle of the rock star in general. Witness the generation of young people who tuned in, turned on and dropped out.

There is no question in my mind that if their parents had insisted on and enforced basic standards of separation in their homes, their children would not have listened to the rock in the first place. Moreover, they would not have tried to mimic their hair and dress styles. There are definite consequences to your outlook on the matter of separation from the world.

Christian parents, just don't allow the current fad of dress and hair. It most likely has come out of the subculture of the world's music and its stars. If you want your kids to idolize that bunch and live like them, then let them listen to their music. They soon will dress and style themselves after them, but realize that they are conforming themselves to the world and the things in the world. Be prepared to face the consequences that surely will come in mid or late adolescence.

We do not have many non-Christian friends that we are close to. I do, though, think of a family we have been friends with for several decades. We have tried repeatedly to lead them to Christ, but they have steadfastly hid behind their "religion." Be that as it may, we have watched them raise their children. These people are college educated, professional people. They are decent, law-abiding, cultured people. They are both respected in their community and both hold responsible and respected positions.

We also watched them allow and encourage their son to get into "music." Of course, that was a rock band. Although he never amounted to anything as a musician, he certainly became engrossed with the rock culture. Though the rest of his family are proceeding to develop as decent business and professional people in their own right, this particular guy is a flop in life. He is intelligent, good hearted, and just a nice guy. He has been raised in a good home as far as the world is concerned. However, the rock 'n roll culture he so imbibed as a teenager and young adult has caused him to essentially be a zero in life. He struggles to hold minimal jobs and has bounced around like a ping pong ball. The fact is, the principle of separation even for unsaved people would have helped that family greatly.

Do yourselves and your children a favor. Get as far from the world and the things of the world as you possibly can. Then, replace those things with the things of God and godly living. You will never regret it!

Chapter 7 - Principles to Practice

There are several undergirding principles in training children and developing Christian character. First, my firm conviction is that the issues of life are fundamentally spiritual and not psychological. I have appealed very little to psychology in general and have appealed none to behavioral psychology. There is a legitimate place for clinical psychology. However, in an individual having normal mental capacity, the problems of behavior are fundamentally spiritual, not psychological.

That leads me to the second undergirding principle in training your children to turn out right. That is the appeal to Scripture for virtually every aspect of the training of our children. Most Bible believing Christians accept God's Word as sufficient for not only *faith* (which pertains to doctrine), but also for *practice* (which is

117

among other things, day-to-day Christian living). Somehow we have been led to believe that all we need to do is turn to modern psychology for the answers to training our children. Maybe that is part of the problem.

I have often wondered how God's people managed to get along before the advent of modern psychology when all they had was the Bible. By the same token, we do not see many John or Charles Wesleys today. Neither do we see many John Bunyans, nor George Whitefields, nor Charles Haddon Spurgeons, nor Adoniram Judsons, nor William Careys, nor Billy Sundays. And the list could go on.

Those poor souls did not have the benefit of modern behavioral psychology to help them along the path of life. All their poor, underprivileged parents had was the Bible to guide them in the rearing of their children. It seems to me, those godly people of a bygone generation did not do too badly in training their children!

The Bible is sufficient for the training of our children. Since the issues of life are spiritual, then there is a need for spiritual guidance and authority in the training of our children. That infallible Guide is none other than the inerrant, verbally inspired Word of God. When Paul wrote to Timothy in II Timothy 3:15-17, he pointed out that the Scriptures were able to make him *"wise unto salvation."* He also pointed out that they were profitable for reproof, correction, and instruction in righteous behavior. The goal was that the man of God might be perfect (literally "complete"), *"thoroughly furnished unto all good works."* Parents, that truth is for more than just preachers. It is for our children and how we train them as well.

Modern behavioral psychology changes its theories and solutions to problems about every 10 or 15 years. The Word of God has never changed. It just stands. Heaven and earth may pass away, but the Word of God will live and abide forever. It is profitable *"for reproof, for correction, for instruction in righteousness."* Therefore, it is all that we need as the ultimate source book and guide for the training of our families. That is all that the parents of Daniel had. It seems to me they did a fairly good job of training Daniel.

The Practice of Godliness

The concept of godliness is woven throughout the Word of God. Paul wrote Timothy to exercise himself unto godliness (I Timothy 4:7-8). *"For bodily exercise profiteth little: but godliness is profitable unto all things, having promise of the life that now is, and of that which is to come."*

In I Timothy 6:11, Paul urged Timothy to pursue not only righteousness, but also godliness along with other spiritual virtues. Peter wrote how we ought to add godliness to the development of our Christian life (II Peter 1:6). Paul wrote to Titus and urged him to live in a godly fashion in this present world (Titus 2:12). The Psalmist told how God has *"set apart him that is godly for Himself"* (Psalm 4:3). It appears that God views godliness as something that is important. We are commanded to be godly and to add it to our character. The Bible says that it is profitable far on into eternity. God will specially set aside the godly for Himself. I do not know about you, but that sounds important to me.

Now, what does that have to do with training our children? Well, a significant goal for our children ought to be that they are godly. Over the years, I have had parents plead when their children were in some sort of difficulty, "But Junior is a good kid," or "My kids are good kids." Well, that may be. My question is, "Are they godly?" It seems that we have raised a generation of Christian young people who are good kids, but not godly. Godliness will not only preclude the various problems

119

alluded to thus far in this book, it will also develop into our children the qualities that God has intended for His people.

Being good may be fine as far as the world is concerned, but God has a far higher standard for our children—that they be godly. Ironically, in many of the sad stories I have related throughout this book, those parents would have characterized their children as "good kids." As far as the world's standards are concerned, maybe they were. But they were not godly. Genuine godliness would have eliminated the majority of the heartaches.

Paul wrote to Titus that the grace of God which bringeth salvation also teaches us that, *"denying ungodliness and worldly lusts, we should live soberly, righteously, and godly, in this present world"* Titus 2:11-12. Godliness covers a fairly broad spectrum. Much of what we have dealt with thus far touches upon godliness. Now we will look at additional areas that pertain to godliness.

The Practice of Faithfulness

That which is profound is usually simple. Let us look at a simple principle which at the same time is profound—faithfulness to the things of God. When an entire family is faithful to the things of God it will have a profound impact on how their children develop spiritually.

The Bible is replete with references to faithfulness. Jesus wrote to the church at Smyrna, *"Be thou faithful unto death, and I will give thee a crown of life"* (Revelation 2:10). In Proverbs 28:20 we read, *"A faithful man shall abound with blessings."* Dad, how can you ignore a promise of blessing for you and your family? Any time a father is blessed, it almost automatically will flow on to the children. Notice that the criteria of the promised blessing here is faithfulness.

The author of Hebrews wrote that we as New Testament Christians are not to forsake *"the assembling of ourselves together"* (Hebrews 10:25). The word for "church" in the Greek New Testament *(ecclessia)* literally means "a called out assembly." When Hebrews 10:25 speaks of not forsaking the assembling together of God's people, it clearly is speaking of the meeting of the local church.

I have had the privilege to be a third generation, fundamental Baptist preacher. My immediate spiritual lineage dates back almost 100 years. Though I am less than half that old, it has always been the firm practice in our family to be present whenever there was a meeting going on in our local church.

The policy in my home, in my parents' home, and in my grandparents' home was simple. Any time the church door was open, we were there. That meant Sunday school on Sunday morning. That meant, of course, the Sunday morning worship service and the Sunday evening service. That meant the mid-week service; and if there were special meetings, we were there.

The only exceptions to that policy were if we were too sick to go or if the weather was such that the church service had been called off altogether. Both of those eventualities were rare. If there was a scheduled meeting of the local church, we all were there: Mom, Dad, and kids. Always! I do not mention that to brag. I mention that because I believe that is the way God intended it to be.

You see, the Bible says, to *"Seek ye first the kingdom of God and his righteousness"* (Matthew 6:33). That means that the things of God are to be the first priority in our lives. If the local church, the body of Christ, is assembling, then I must seek that first. It takes priority over anything else in my life.

Let me just add that the local church of the New Testament is God's primary and specific work in this age. It is the body of Christ. And if I, as a Christian, am to be faithful to Jesus Christ, then I had best be faithful to His body and His work.

121

You may protest, "That is a bit too much. I mean, preacher, there are other things in life besides church, you know." Well, my friend, if you want your children to turn out as godly young people with straight Christian character, you had best be faithful to the local church. And I mean really faithful.

Let me use an illustration that might seem rather narrow. How many times must a spouse commit adultery to be considered unfaithful? Should our faithfulness to the Lord be any less considered?

My grandparents practiced the aforementioned policy. Both of their daughters wound up marrying preachers and have both spent around 50 years in the ministry each. My parents practiced this policy and all three of their children headed off into the ministry. We have practiced this policy in our home; and though our daughters have yet to finish college, they certainly are pointed in that direction.

You say, "Well, that is not my goal for *my* children." Dear friend, you had best shoot for God's will for your children. Maybe God will not place them into the ministry. What a tragedy, though, if your children miss God's will for their lives because you as a parent were sloppy and careless in the matter of faithfulness.

Incidentally, there is no higher calling than for God to place one into His work in a full-time way. The overtones of that will last for all eternity. We have sought to groom our children for God's work. Nothing will make us happier, if that is what they in fact do. And the practice of faithfulness in our home to the things of God has been a considerable factor in that training.

When we went on vacation, we looked for a fundamental Bible-preaching church within driving distance (and there usually was one). Then, we were faithful to each service of that local church. That meant everything on Sunday and on Wednesday night. During the course of my ministry, I have pastored in three places. As it turned out, each of those places was a tourist

122

destination. When we were in Florida, people came there in the winter. As I have pastored in Minnesota, people vacation in our area in the summer.

It has been interesting to watch Christians on vacation. We have watched pastors come to town for a week or two and all we have seen of them was for one Sunday morning service. Others come to the area and every time the church door is open, they are present, even on vacation. The same diverse pattern holds true for Christian lay people.

I am mindful of a retired couple who have never ceased to bless me. They were well-known across the land throughout their many years in the ministry. When I was a young man, they had a profound influence on my life. They own a summer cabin on a lake about 30 miles from our church. They are well up in years, and it is probably a 45 minute drive in to our church. Yet, if they are in the area, they are present . . . Sunday morning, Sunday evening and the mid-week service. And they have the courtesy and grace to let us know if for some reason they are going to be away and cannot be present.

What a wonderful testimony to their Savior. As long-time servants of God, they still are faithful. They have taken the injunction of Revelation 2:10 seriously, *"Be thou faithful unto death."* By the way, their only daughter is faithfully serving the Lord as a missionary school teacher.

However, the book of I Samuel records some detail about the life of Eli, the high priest, who was not so faithful. Eli will be eternally infamous in the annals of God's people for being a man whose sons were a disgrace. They deeply besmirched the testimony of the tabernacle and its ministry. Read about them in I Samuel 2:12-17 and 22-25. They embezzled at the tabernacle and extorted from God's people. They even had the unmitigated gall to commit fornication and adultery with women who came to the tabernacle. They were not nice guys.

But notice how God evaluated their father, Eli, in I Samuel 2:35. *"And I will raise me up a faithful priest . . . ."* Notice the implication that Eli was not faithful in the things of God. I do not think it is a coincidence about how his sons turned out. Unfaithfulness is another form of spiritual inconsistency. It, more often than not, will breed spiritual rebellion in our children.

Once again the principle of both mother and father being consistent and faithful reoccurs. It takes both pulling the load together. If one or the other, mom or dad, are not faithful to the things of God, beware. The harvest will come in your children. And you will not be happy when it comes.

On the one hand, I think of a dear godly couple we knew well. They both were advanced in years. He was in his early 80's and she in her late 70's, but they were faithful. They lived in Minnesota, and winters in Minnesota are world renowned for their severity. Yet this dear couple never missed church services, even in the winter. When it got so that he could no longer drive much, then she drove.

I remember one winter Sunday when it started snowing about the time church let out at noon. It snowed all afternoon and on into the evening. I suppose by church time Sunday evening, we had received eight inches of new snow, and it was still snowing. The crowd was thin that evening, but this dear couple was there. Oh, by the way, all of their adult children to this day are godly Christians living for the Lord.

Likewise, I think of another couple. Like those mentioned above, they too were elderly, and they too were faithful. No matter what, they were just there. When the time came that they could no longer drive to church, particularly in the winter, they had some one pick them up. Until the time they went into a nursing home and became senile, they were just faithful to the things of God . . . even unto death. Their children, to this day, are a lovely testimony of Jesus Christ and His grace. It pays to be faithful, if for no other reason than how our children will develop spiritually.

However, let me once again share with you the other side of the coin. I have witnessed numerous families where the matter of faithfulness to the things of God is forgotten when other interests and pursuits are at hand.

I think of one guy who was fairly faithful, 90% of the time. He was present for most of the services of the church with two exceptions. When deer hunting season rolled around **every** year, I knew where he would be each Sunday of hunting season. Though he was a deacon and Sunday School teacher, come deer hunting season, he was out hunting all day Sunday.

Then when camping season came in the summer, we could just count on this guy being gone for about three or four Sundays because he was out camping over the weekends. Now in the main, this fellow was a good man and otherwise relatively faithful. But when hunting and camping time showed up, he no longer sought first the kingdom of God. Not unpredictably, he had major trouble with his children. In fact, some of the sad and sordid stories found elsewhere in this book involved some of his children.

I think of another family. Both the parents loved the Lord. They were active in the church and were for the most part rather faithful. But again, when camping season showed up each year, they just disappeared from church for about a half of the summer. They were out camping. Now camping is not wrong. Over the years I have loved to go in the Boundary Waters Canoe Area Wilderness along the Minnesota and Canadian border to paddle and camp. However, we **always** ordered the trip so that it was not on the Lord's day. Well anyway, this couple who otherwise was a real asset to the church, sure enough, had trouble with one of their kids, big time. But they just could not see the inconsistency in their lives. Their child did; however, and that young person completely turned away from the things of God.

There was once a time when public schools avoided scheduling activities and events that might conflict with church schedules. In the Midwestern community in which I grew up, the local school district grudgingly avoided scheduling extra-curricular events and activities on Wednesday night because for many people in town, that was "church night." In a similar way, there were never any school activities or functions scheduled on Sunday evenings because a percentage of the community, though small, went to church on Sunday evening.

I do not know how that school district handles things today, but in this area, there routinely are events that conflict with Sunday evening and Wednesday evening services. It presents a dilemma for people who have children in the public schools. Should they be faithful to the things of God, or should they skip church and support the school activity? They often find themselves over a barrel. If they put their foot down, then the coach says that their son or daughter cannot be on the team. Perhaps that is one more reason to consider a Christian school.

As a pastor, I am concerned for our young people who are in such situations. If they are going to be involved in any sort of extra curricular activities, they run the risk of having such conflicts. Then they have to make a decision of quitting the activity or of being faithful to the things of God. It is a hard dilemma for young people. Of course, they would be better served by being enrolled in a Christian school for this and other reasons, but sometimes that is not always a viable option.

Another variant of the foregoing matter is that of staying home from church to do school work. Over the years I have heard parents use the following excuse for why their children were not in a Sunday night or Wednesday night church service. "They had too much home work to do." Priorities do not conflict. School work is important, but the things of God are more important.

Remember, our Lord said to seek first the kingdom of God. In my opinion, that means the things of God get first priority.

The truth is, if children come right home from school and get right on to school work, they will have time for that hour and a half before an evening service or church function. We make time for what we *want* to do. I believe that God will honor a student who honors Him by being faithful in putting Him first.

Apart from that, there is a much deeper significance involved here. When we allow other things to take priority over the things of God, we are tacitly teaching our children that the Lord really is not most important in their lives. School work, school activities, and perhaps, recreational activities are what are really important and have first priority. That is serious business, and that attitude will undermine spiritual character for years to come. Now, you can teach that the Lord comes first all you want, but what you give priority to, indeed, will speak the loudest.

I attended a public high school more than thirty years ago. I was very active in the concert band and to some degree excelled in it. As it happened, the high school band director also was the director of the local municipal band. It was a semi-professional organization made up of fairly accomplished local musicians and a few high school students. During the summer months, the municipal band would give a concert in the park every Sunday evening at the park pavilion. It was a typical Midwestern, small town event, but it was fairly well attended. It was an honor for a high school student to be asked to play in that band. (Furthermore, the musicians were paid for each performance.)

Between my junior and senior year in high school, I was asked to play in the municipal band. For my part, I was all for it. But Dad said, "No, you belong in the Lord's house on the Lord's day." That was that. I was not too happy about the decision at the time, but in retrospect, I am glad that I had a father who had the courage of conviction to stick to principle and force me to be faithful to the things of God. That principle has stuck with me all through life. I am confident it has had a bearing upon how my own children have turned out.

Both of our daughters have pretty much earned their way through college. When they turned sixteen, both of them went out and found jobs in a rather tight job market. We have watched as other young people in the church were hired, and inevitably they would be scheduled to work on Sundays and Wednesday evenings. We often heard the refrain, "I won't be in church Sunday; I have to work."

We counselled our girls to specify up front when applying for work that they could not work on Sundays or on Wednesday evenings, because they had church services then. People said, "Well, they'll never get much work that way." But the fact of the matter is, they have never lacked for a job. God has provided them the means to largely earn their way through college in a community that is not overflowing with employment opportunities.

Even when they have come home mid-term or in the summer, they have requested of employers that they be allowed to be faithful to church on Sundays and Wednesday evenings. Surprisingly, their employers have cheerfully cooperated. In fact, while working under that arrangement, our younger daughter was the first 17-year-old in the region, and perhaps the country, to be promoted into management working for a large, well-known, national chain of stores. Though they have never had an abundance of cash, they both are paying their way through college. God has blessed them for their faithfulness.

Mom and Dad, set an example of faithfulness; then see to it that your children are faithful. They may not always be thrilled with the idea, especially when they have to forego an activity they like. But it will help instill a pattern and conviction that will be a blessing for all involved for years to come.

In I Samuel 2:30, God's Word says, *"For them that honor me, I will honor . . . ."* Honoring the Lord as parents will bring God's honor to your family and children. Teaching your children to honor the Lord by honest to goodness faithfulness to the Lord,

128

will bring His honor upon them. You will never go wrong to honor the Lord, neither will your children.

Have you ever wondered how Daniel would have reacted as a captive student in Babylon if his parents had compromised the principle of faithfulness? I submit that we would not be naming our children Daniel to this day. That which made Daniel a man of such sterling character was his determination to be faithful and honor the Lord no matter what the cost.

Teach faithfulness. Lead by example. Be consistent therein. See to it that your children are faithful throughout the years they live under your roof. The difference will be known on into eternity.

The Practice of Devotions

Here is another practice crucial for establishing godliness in our children, the practice of family devotions or family altar. Neither term appears as such in the Bible, but the concept certainly does. These terms refer to the same thing, the daily instruction of children by their parents in the things of God.

Deuteronomy 6:7 (also 11:19) says, *"And thou shalt teach them diligently unto thy children, and shalt talk of them when thou sittest in thine house, and when thou walkest by the way, and when thou liest down, and when thou risest up."* The Bible clearly teaches that we as parents are to teach our children the things of God. Others, such as Sunday school teachers, church workers, and Christian school teachers can be of assistance. However, the primary task of teaching our children the things of God is the responsibility of the parents.

One of the most effective ways to do so is to establish a time each day when we sit down and directly teach our children. This is what I refer to as family devotions. Over the years, we utilized our family devotions as a forum to teach our girls about

129

salvation. Then, after they trusted Christ, we used our family devotions to teach principles of Christian character such as righteousness and the self-discipline to do right. We used this forum to instill other principles and godliness in general.

Family schedules will vary from home to home. We found, in the main, that breakfast time was our best bet for having all the family together. Therefore, we sought to maintain a time each morning at the breakfast table to teach biblical principles and pray together. There were times when for one reason or another that time did not work. Therefore, we rescheduled that day for either lunch or the evening meal. The Bible is not specific in the *when*, but it does instruct us in the *what*. Set a time that will work in your home. Then stick to it religiously. If you do have complications, then reschedule for another time, but do it, and keep on doing it.

As a pastor, it has been my experience that many people struggle with family devotions because they do not have a simple and practical way to do it over the long term. Over the years we have allowed distribution of devotional booklets through the church. But I have always cautioned our people to never allow the devotional booklet to be a substitute for personal Bible reading. I have cautioned them to never let it be a substitute for actually going to the Word in family devotions. View the booklet as a supplement, but never allow it to take the place of the Bible itself.

However, many good Christian people are just not sure of how to use the Bible directly for family devotions. Let me offer a list of tips for effective, on-going family devotions.

1. Have a purpose. I think many people view family altar or devotions as something they know they should do, but they really do not have any specific purpose in mind. We viewed our family time in the Word and prayer with several distinct purposes.

Our main goal was to teach the Word of God to our children according to the needs in their lives. When they were little, they needed to understand the various facets concerning salvation. As explained in an earlier chapter, we taught them about **the need of salvation.** Teach them who Jesus Christ is. Teach them what He did on Calvary and how one can be saved.

In their beginner and preschool years, that is not all that we dwelt upon in family devotions, but it certainly was one goal among several. Week after week we would touch upon one thing or another that pertained to salvation. We would talk about sin and go to such simple places as Romans 3:23. We would talk about what sin was and if we sinned. We would relate it to daily things such as disobeying mom or dad, fighting with their sister, or lying. Other times, we would talk about the consequences of sin such as in Romans 6:23. We would attempt (at times with difficulty) to explain what hell was and who was going there. Other times, we would explain about John 3:16 and about Jesus. We would talk on other days about Jesus dying on the cross and Jesus rising from the dead. We would talk about where Jesus is now. Then, on other days we would talk about how to be saved.

Week after week we laid a foundation of biblical truth. We asked questions to draw out the girls and seek their understanding of what was being taught. Where they were unclear we would go back over those areas. Little by little, they came to understand the entire concept of salvation and the work of Christ for them. Then came the sweet times when they, of their own volition, asked Christ to save them.

Another major goal we had in mind for our family devotions was the instilling of **Christian character.** As you may recall from the chapter on righteousness, Christian character may be defined as the self-discipline to do what is right. Therefore, we spent many, many mornings looking at Bible verses dealing with righteousness. Many a time we would instill into our children, "We always do what is right . . . ." If they heard that once, they heard it a thousand times.

A third goal was to instill specific commands and principles pertaining to **righteousness** and Christian character. For example, one of the first applications of righteousness was the admonition in Ephesians 6, *"Children obey your parents in the Lord, for this is right."* We then would also point out that it is not right to lie. It was right to be kind to your sister. We would frequently refer to Ephesians 4:32 where Paul admonished, *"And be ye kind one to another, tenderhearted, forgiving one another."* Even preacher's kids would fight and be unkind to each other. The Bible is full of practical day-to-day applications of righteousness. As the children grew older, we selected ideas that were commensurate with their age level.

2. Have a plan. Now perhaps you are thinking, "Well, you have been trained in college and in seminary. It won't be so easy for us." That is probably true. Nevertheless, most Christian parents can explain the plan of salvation in childlike terms. You can take a verse at a time such as Romans 3:23 and Romans 6:23 or John 3:16 and talk about it. It may mean a little mental preparation ahead of time, but are not your children and their spiritual development important?

In the matter of teaching about righteousness, the books of Psalms and Proverbs overflow with references. I have counselled our people over the years to read through Psalms and Proverbs in their own personal Bible reading. Then I have encouraged them to underline and take note of the many references to righteousness therein.

There are 31 chapters in Proverbs. That is roughly one for each day of the month. As our girls got older, we followed the practice of going to the Proverb that corresponded to the day of the month. We then would find a verse that pertained to righteousness (or whatever else we wanted to teach). From my earlier personal Bible reading, I had marked the majority of poignant places that referred to righteousness. It was then quite easy, on any given day, to find such a reference by just turning to the chapter of the day.

A similar procedure in Psalms was to take each day of the month and multiply it by five. Therefore, on the tenth day of the month for example, I would go to the vicinity of Psalms 50 and quickly peruse what I already had marked in personal Bible reading. Almost immediately, I could find a verse to talk about for a few minutes in family devotions. Again, we tried to focus upon areas of Christian character such as righteousness and obedience to God. It always was directly from the Bible and our children knew that. They knew that dad was teaching them biblical principles, and they knew the Bible was God's Word.

Then, each day after having taken a few minutes to discuss a short portion of scripture, we would all pray. We would coach the children when they were small on what to say, but nevertheless, they participated. As they got older their prayers became more mature.

3. Keep it simple. Over the years I have observed various families and their attempts to have family devotions. Frequently, the scenario went something like this. As a result of someone preaching about it, mom and dad would get all fired up about having family devotions. They would go home and shortly thereafter launch into their new and improved family devotions. They would read Scripture, sing a hymn, memorize a verse, have a prayer list and so forth. It all was quite impressive.

The problem was, after about two weeks of that format, they gave up on the idea. It was too complicated and it took too much preparation time. Inevitably, such plans fizzle out. Then the parents develop a guilt complex. Worse still, they give up on the idea altogether. "I mean we tried and it just did not work for us."

Over the years, we practiced a very simple format. I would read a verse of Scripture and make a few simple comments from it that usually were self-evident within the text. Then everybody would pray together. Say our goal at the time was to explain some aspect of salvation to one of our children. Then I would select some simple verse that illustrated the portion of the plan of salvation we were working at that week.

If our goal was to teach Christian character, I usually would go to Psalms or Proverbs (according to the day of the month). There I would find a verse dealing with righteousness or obedience, or some application thereof. Since I had already marked my Bible extensively in personal Bible study long before, I just looked for one of those marked verses.

One might wonder if we ran out of material. The answer is "No." One of the laws of learning is repetition. And indeed, repetition has been called the mother of learning. As we worked back and forth with the children and their respective needs spiritually, we often repeated at least the basic concepts. Reiterating a principle over again lends itself to positive reenforcement.

View family devotions as a means to several specific ends. Use it as a vehicle to teach your children about salvation and the things that follow salvation. Use it to teach Christian character, specifically the matter of righteousness. Use it to teach other principles of godliness, such as separation from the world, missions, and serving God.

* * *

Before we leave the subject of teaching our children, let us return again to Deuteronomy 6:7. Notice that the passage sets forth *how* we ought to teach the principles of God's Word. *"Thou shalt teach them diligently unto thy children, and shalt talk of them when thou sittest in thine house, and when thou walkest by the way, and when thou liest down, and when thou risest up."* Now, this classic portion of God's word tells us to teach our children the things of God diligently when we sit down. That might be interpreted to mean when we sit down to eat. Hence, the idea of family devotions as we have discussed it.

However, notice also that God has instructed us to teach our children, *"when thou walkest by the way."* The word "way" is a reference to a pathway or highway. It is a reference to when the family, or a portion thereof, is traveling from one place to another. When our girls were small we would drive around town together. (It was before the days of mandatory seat belt laws.) They would stand up on the "hump" behind me in the back seat area. As we drove, we would talk about the things of God. When they were that young, the conversation usually was on various aspects of salvation: the need of it, what Jesus did for us on the cross, and how to be saved. I believe that we were fulfilling the injunction in Deuteronomy 6:7 to teach the things of God as we walked (or drove) in the way.

However, there is more. Notice also that we are instructed to teach the things of God diligently to our children, *"when thou liest down."* In all likelihood that is a reference to bed time. Up until our girls were well into high school, at least one of us parents would go and have prayer with them beside their bed each night. It was a part of the "tucking them in" ritual. But we often would take time to talk a bit about the things of God. In fact, one of the girls got saved during such a bed time prayer session.

Finally, the text instructs us to teach our children when they rise up. Our family devotions as such usually were in the morning. In any event, we made it a point most mornings to make sure that the children had spent time alone with the Lord before they went on with the day.

I believe that God intended our homes be the primary place for the instruction of godliness for our children. Now, of necessity, that demands that we as parents must be on top of things spiritually ourselves. It also implies that we shall have done enough personal Bible study so that we can do rudimentary teaching of it to our children.

The Practice of Love

Another concept endemic to godliness is the matter of love. Though we have touched upon this earlier, let us look at it once more. Jesus said in John 15:12, *"This is my commandment, That ye love one another, as I have loved you."* The New Testament fairly overflows with references to God's people being people of love.

Curiously, the Bible has little to say about parents loving their children. I believe the reason for this is that God has created within us a natural instinct to love our children. I have never met a Christian parent who did not love his or her children. (Some people in the world have been so distorted by sin that they have lost that God-given love for their children.) Nevertheless, it is important that our homes be an aquarium of love. In all your teaching, disciplining, and admonishing of your children, always season it liberally with love.

See that your children have no doubt whatsoever that you love them. Tell them you love them. Show physical affection in an appropriate fashion such as hugs and discreet kisses. Always be there when they need you. Never be too busy for their school functions or programs. Love them even more than you love yourself.

Not only is it right to love your children, it will enable you to most effectively teach and train them. When they unquestionably know you love them, they know that you have their best interests at heart. Mom and dad, I do not doubt for one minute that you love your children. My point only is that you are careful to express it. Moreover, do it consistently and regularly. It certainly pertains to godliness.

136

Chapter 8 - Consistency Is the Key

My ministry has been almost entirely working with families or their children. During that time, I have observed some basic trends that seem to repeat themselves. Although an individual can break out of a family pattern by the grace of God and overcome traits of parents, I have observed a direct correlation between how children turn out spiritually and the spiritual temperature of their parents.

Twenty years ago, I had the privilege of working with the youth of the church. Later, I worked with the young couples in the church. At the same time, my wife and I worked together in the large children's church program of the church. Then we started the Christian school. Again, I worked with families and their children.

It was a unique experience. I came to know the younger children in the children's church program. I also knew the teenagers, having been the youth pastor for several years. In working with the young couples of the church, I got to know the parents of many of these same young people.

Spirituality and character in the children and teenagers closely parallelled the degree of spiritual maturity and character evident in their parents. I came to learn that when the Bible spoke about reaping what we sow in Galatians 6, it likely had an application to our offspring.

We come right back to one of the basic premises of this book. *The issues of life are fundamentally spiritual.* There are few things more basic to life than our children. How we as parents live spiritually will profoundly affect our children. It therefore behooves us as parents to set the highest example we possibly can. The Apostle Paul wrote to *"Be thou an example of the believer"* in I Timothy 4:12. As much is caught as is taught.

Carnal parents tend to produce carnal children. Spiritual parents tend to rear spiritual children. Compromising parents tend to produce compromising offspring. Disciplined parents tend to produce the same.

Let us go a step further. Let us picture a hypothetical family. In this family, one parent is seeking to live for the Lord and serve Him. This parent is genuinely spiritual. But the other parent is floating spiritually. The spiritual results in their children will likely be disastrous. You will recall some of the horror stories mentioned earlier in this book. In most of those cases, one parent had a perceptible spiritual weakness while the other did not.

In American society today, there are far more homes with single parents than I care to admit. And some of these folks are Christian people. In some of these cases, children seem to do as well as their counterparts in stable nuclear families.

If you are a single parent because of divorce or other domestic upheaval, you still should pay heed to this chapter. The principles will be much the same for your situation. However, for the purposes of this chapter, we will assume a traditional, nuclear family with both parents married and living together.

A more subtle situation is where the marriage is stable, but one parent is living for the Lord, and the other really is not. In such cases, beware. Trouble is just over the horizon. *"Be not deceived; God is not mocked: for whatsoever a man soweth, that shall he also reap. For he that soweth to his flesh shall of the flesh reap corruption; but he that soweth to the Spirit shall of the Spirit reap life everlasting"* (Galatians 6:7-8).

Mom and Dad, the major harvest of life will be in our children. We will reap in them what we have sown spiritually in our own lives. When there has been sowing to the flesh, the harvest will be bitter and corrupt. When we sow to the Spirit, the harvest will be eternal and sweet. This directly affects the matter of how our children will turn out! Again, the inconsistency of just *one* parent can be the spiritual undoing of the children.

Unfortunately, children tend to gravitate spiritually in the direction of the less spiritual parent. Children also tend to amplify in their own lives the spiritual weaknesses of the weaker of their parents. Therefore, it behooves us as parents to live to the highest spiritual level we possibly can.

Testimonies That Talk

Let me share again some examples of people I have personally known and ministered to. Notice the correlation between the parents' spiritual consistency and how their children developed spiritually. In each case, the names used are fictitious. The events described have taken place over a period of 25 years in four different states. The stories are true, but the names and some details have been changed to disguise identity.

I'll call him Jack. I well remember the weekend Jack and his wife were saved. The next day they walked the aisle in church, publicly professing their new faith in Jesus Christ. Jack began to grow in the Lord. His wife, Sue, followed along but not as carefully. Brother Jack began to get involved in serving the Lord in various ministries in the church. He served in the bus ministry and then taught a Sunday school class. He helped in the youth program and was a willing worker whenever there was a church work day.

His wife, however, just sat on her hands spiritually. She wouldn't teach Sunday school when asked. She wouldn't help in various ladies' ministries. She wouldn't go to the ladies' retreats and meetings. Whereas her husband began to immediately separate himself from his worldly habits and entertainments, she made excuses such as, "Well, *I* don't see anything wrong with *that.*" She continued to run around the house and yard in her short shorts and halter top. She continued to play her country western music in the car and around the house.

If her husband had to work on Wednesday evening, no way was she going to drive to church alone (though she drove anywhere she wanted any other time). No way was she going to go to the ladies' Bible study. And, though her husband went out on church visitation from time to time, she did not. To be honest, she may never have really been born again, though I have no way of knowing that for sure. If she was saved, she certainly was not spiritual. But her husband was. He really tried. More than once he came to the altar at invitation time with a tender heart, making a decision for Jesus Christ.

How did the children in this family turn out? Even though both of them were in the Christian school, I don't think either of them is living for the Lord today. One by one, the children gravitated to the spiritual inconsistency and carnality of their mother. In fact, the spiritual weakness of that woman has been amplified and multiplied in their lives. Though I have lost track of one of them, I know that at least the other has been in deep trouble. Both parents have been grieved in their hearts.

* * *

In another family, Jane was from a rough background. She made a dramatic turn about in her life. To the glory of God, she had been genuinely born again. She made a point of being in every service she possibly could. She insisted that her children be faithful with her. She was not an infrequent visitor with tears to the altar at invitation time. She helped in whatever ministry she was able. She tithed of the income from her part-time job.

If she had to work when a service was scheduled, she made a point of seeing that her children were picked up for church. She wanted to place her children into the Christian school, but finances just didn't allow it. Her husband likewise made a profession of faith. He attended church some, but he certainly wasn't faithful. He still clung to his cigarettes and his beer. He professed to be a Christian, but he still indulged in watching coarse TV programs even in front of his children. His wife was trying her hardest spiritually and he was coasting at best.

As the children began to reach adolescence, they began to be drawn into the world. Their mother frantically prayed and sought help from the church. But sadly, one parent had allowed himself to sow to his flesh. The harvest began to come in. Four out of their five children are in the world today and are certainly not living for the Lord.

* * *

Another couple was deeply involved in the church. That church had many boards and committees. Some people in the church had the idea that serving the Lord was synonymous with sitting on these boards and committees. The husband was on several committees and was a board member. The wife was on several committees and chaired one. They were gung ho committee people seeking to run the church through the various boards and committees they were on.

When a new pastor arrived, he recommended that the church revise its constitution to eliminate the seemingly endless board and committee meetings. The recommendation ground its way through the prescribed channels and the church unanimously approved the changes. Now, this fine lady no longer had any committee meetings to attend or chair. She soon became disgruntled and was in silent rebellion against the pastor.

The rebellion and developing disloyalty to spiritual leadership, though more or less quiet outside the home, was aired openly in the home. Everybody in that household knew that Mom had come to detest the pastor. Now, pastors are not always right, and this pastor has made his share of mistakes, but there is a greater principle of divinely ordained leadership. Overt rebellion against such, as a rule, is wrong, and it can produce even greater problems when your children learn of it. In this case, the pastor went to these people and asked their forgiveness for any wrong inflicted on them. They did not respond well.

When a parent becomes rebellious against scriptural leadership, his attitude is going to rub off on his children. Usually, there are other spiritual problems attendant with rebellion, and this case was no exception. There was fudging on matters of separation and problems of fighting within the family. It was not long before one of the children in the family began to rebel in the Christian school.

Disciplinary problems began to accelerate to such a degree that the student was expelled from the school. That caused a total blow up with the parents. But what they did not see nor seemingly understand was that the rebellion of one parent in particular had been all that was needed to spark outward rebellion in one of their children. It came at the most crucial time—in the mid and late adolescent years. That poor young adult has bounced around ever since.

* * *

Years ago, Frank and Betty placed their children in our Christian school. Frank was a faithful Christian. As he was given responsibilities in the church, he faithfully executed his duties.

He attended the services. In fact, he could have been considered one of the pillars of the church.

However, his wife Betty always seemed to have some excuse for missing the services. One week she wasn't feeling well. The next week, one of the children wasn't feeling well. Then another week Aunt Ethyl would be visiting and she had to stay home and fix meals for her. Then Betty would come to church for a couple of weeks, but after that she had a headache on Sunday morning. When Frank occasionally had to work on a Sunday, Betty said she just didn't have any way to get to church.

Then the next Sunday, one of the children had the sniffles, and she surely didn't want him to give it to one of the other boys or girls at church. Therefore, she stayed home with him. After that, she would attend for a week or two, and then the cycle would start all over again. She thought that the pastor was too strict with all this business about "separation" and "standards." Her mom had not brought *her* up that way. Surely, those things weren't *that* bad. Besides, all the neighbor kids did those kinds of things and they were good kids.

Later, one of Frank and Betty's children announced that he was old enough to make his own decisions. "When someone is 16, he can make his own decisions." Having said that, her son announced that he had decided that he was too old to go to church any more. Therefore, he was going to quit, and his attitude was, "you can't make me go!!"

How could a faithful man like Frank have something like this happen to his family? Sadly, these children have disappointed their parents and in one case utterly broken their hearts. These parents just cannot understand how their children would turn out that way. "I mean they were good kids. They were brought up better than that. We even sent them to the Christian school."

"Be not deceived; God is not mocked: for whatsoever a man [or woman] soweth, that shall he also reap." Betty had made every excuse she could think of to skip any spiritual

responsibility in the things of God. Is it any wonder her children followed in her footsteps? However, the children did so openly and without excuses. *"Be thou an example of the believer."*

* * *

Fred and June loved the Lord. They were about as active in the church as a couple could be. At one time they had considered going into the ministry. Their goal for their three sons was that they go into full-time Christian service. These young people had as much potential to go into full-time Christian service as any of the Christian young people I have ever known. They even went out with their parents on church and Sunday school visitation. They loved to be involved in God's work.

Little by little, Fred's budding company began to grow. As he spent more and more time with his company, he began to let the things of God fall by the way side. He had not gone off into any kind of deep sin; he just did not have time to serve the Lord like he once did. Now Fred not only did not have time to work in the church, he no longer had time to even be faithful to the services. In fact, he missed more than he was present, and it got to the point where he basically quit attending. Business was good, and things were happening. Money was being made big time.

As Fred slid away from faithfulness and service, he began to mess around with the things of the world. There was nothing overt, but he nevertheless was flirting with fringes of the world in entertainments and enjoyments. His wife, June, began to follow suit. She started working at the company and, though she never quit going to church, she became too busy to serve the Lord as she once had.

Not one of those fine boys entered full-time Christian service, though they probably had more potential to serve Jesus Christ than most young men I have known. Today, they are Sunday morning Christians, and one boy does not attend church at all. Dad set the example, and the entire family followed his lead.

* * *

I think of Charlie and Joan who had been in the church for years. They were fairly faithful. Joan taught Sunday school and Bible school. She faithfully went to ladies' Bible studies and even went out on visitation for the church. Charlie, however, never attended prayer meeting. He frequently skipped the Sunday evening service to go fishing or putter around the house. He grumbled about giving. He watched just about anything he felt like on the TV, even when the children were around.

I don't think I ever recall Charlie responding to an altar call for anything—rededication, Bible reading, getting right with God —anything. On widely separated occasions, winds of revival swept across the church and virtually the entire church would be at the altar at invitation time, but not Charlie. He just stood there with his arms crossed high on his chest.

That kind of example *does* influence the children. Once again the children gravitated to the pattern of the less spiritual parent. Of Joan and Charlie's four children, not one of them today is living for the Lord. One has been in serious trouble with the law. Another has had a track record of moral problems, and the others, though not outwardly in any type of serious sin, are just duds spiritually. Even though the family went to church, the children saw right through the inconsistent example of their father. As a result, they rebelled against the things of God. That does not justify or condone it, but it ought to give pause to professing Christian parents who are lukewarm spiritually and live an inconsistent Christian life.

* * *

George and Mary were active in the church. Mary was a faithful, quiet woman who taught Sunday school and worked wherever she was needed. George was an outgoing fellow who went in spurts. When he was up, he was up; and when he was down, he was down. He admitted that he just never was consistent in daily Bible reading and prayer. He lived for fellowship, but because of his inconsistent daily devotions, George stayed spiritually shallow.

It is impossible to walk in the Spirit apart from the Word of God and regular prayer time. As a result, though George loved the Lord and loved his church, he more often than not walked in the flesh. His fuse was short enough to be measured in millimeters; and when his temper ignited, it was like a howitzer going off. He often would come back and apologize later for his display of temper and foul spirit; but all too often, the damage was done.

His three children witnessed this at home. They knew how inconsistent their father was. At church, he often was on his feet giving a testimony on Wednesday nights. They knew he often was involved in various ministries of the church. But they also knew how moody and temperamental he was at home. They knew of the loud fights and verbal abuse that came from his mouth.

Children and teenagers are very perceptive of inconsistency and hypocrisy. Perhaps, because they are required to be under authority, they subconsciously scrutinize those over them. In the case of George and Mary, the children again gravitated to the lower denominator in their home spiritually. One of the children, even before he was out of the Christian school, was heading for trouble. That particular child, through deep moral sin and much trouble, grieved the parents. The other children have just faded away spiritually and are not serving the Lord in any fashion.

Mom and Dad, we do reap what we sow, and the harvest often comes through the children.

* * *

I think of Dave and Sally. Dave was truly one of the pillars of the church. His testimony in the community was exemplary. His leadership in the church was strong and loyal. He was a faithful tither, and he was a deacon in the church. His wife also tended to be a leader among the ladies of the church. She was faithful in many ways.

Yet, she had a razor-sharp tongue. She was known on occasion to have showdowns at church with someone with whom she was angry. Usually, it was not hard to know what the squabble was all about. The volume level was such that many could hear. Family fights at home were legendary in the neighborhood. Yet, she would later get over it, apologize, and go on from there. However, the damage had been done.

This couple, in the main, were sweet, loyal, spiritual and just good people. Yet, there was enough spiritual inconsistency to affect their children. Though all of them graduated from the Christian school (not without intervals of expulsion along the way), three of the four kids slipped off the deep end into sin as soon as they were on their own. During the crucial formative years, they had witnessed the inconsistencies and blow ups. The sowing to the flesh indeed brought a harvest of corruption. Again, the children had gravitated to the lowest common denominator spiritually in their home.

It Can Be Done

To this point the examples have been negative. And sadly in my experience, there have probably been more negative outcomes than genuinely spiritual and godly outcomes in Christian homes. That is profoundly tragic.

On the brighter side, let me share with you some positive examples. Though I am tempted to use real names at this point, better judgment will preclude that. Let me tell you about families that did turn out young people who today are godly and serving the Lord.

I think of Bob and Jean. They were faithful servants of God. They were loyal to the church and whoever their pastor was.

They tithed faithfully. They were as faithful to the things of God as the hands on the clock. There was genuine spirituality in their persons and throughout their home. They were both students of the Word and were prayer warriors. They were not particularly talented; but they were humble, godly, loyal people. They tried their hardest to do right, particularly in the matter of separation from things of the world. They were authentic in their Christian life and how they deported themselves at home.

As their children graduated from the Christian school, each of them went off to a Christian college. Today, two of them are in full-time Christian service, and the other two are faithful, godly, lay people in their respective churches. Mom and Dad had consistently sown to the Spirit throughout the years. They reaped a lovely and enduring harvest in their children.

* * *

I am mindful of Eldon and Martha. If ever there was a Christian home where there was godly discipline, true spirituality in the parents, and a consistent example of day-to-day Christian living, it was theirs. Their home was just a taste of heaven, in that it was peaceful and godly. It also was godly in that they did not tolerate the corruption of the world in the music or the TV programming they allowed. There was ongoing consistent separation. There was an open example of parents being in the Word and prayer daily. The children not only were taught such, but they saw the consistent example of their parents.

Today, all four of those children are in full-time Christian service either as a pastor, or a missionary, or the wives of such. Mom and Dad had sown to the Spirit, and the pleasant harvest of godly children to this day blesses their hearts. The grandchildren are also being trained in the same pattern.

* * *

My mind goes to the home of John and Gail. Again, they were godly, loyal, humble, spiritual, faithful servants of God. (Now, that may not sound cool to the present generation, but believe me, the proof has been in the pudding in the lives of their children.) I have never known of any inconsistency in the lives of these dear people. They just lived godly, dedicated, faithful, separated, righteous, disciplined lives, and they continue to do so.

Carnal Christians might surmise that they must not have had any fun in their lives. I can assure you their home overflowed with humor and laughter. I have never known them to fight or lose their tempers. Maybe they did, but it surely was not a pattern others could perceive. Their neighbors to this day love them. The people of the church view them as one of the central pillars of the church.

Guess how their children turned out? Though none of them has gone into the ministry or full-time Christian service, each is a stable, faithful, godly young adult. They are a part of their local churches and are willing workers. The consistency and example of their parents reenforced the training they received at home. As a result, they willingly followed their parents' example and willingly received their spiritual training.

* * *

Tom and Jane were pillars of the church. They were sweet of spirit, godly, separated, disciplined, righteous people. They were generous not only in their support of their church, but also in helping others in the community. They were just real. Both of them held positions of leadership in the church, but that does not mean much in the matter of how children turn out. Nevertheless, they were willing servants of Jesus Christ. Both were humble and loyal; both were students of the Word and regular in prayer. They could be counted upon in any way.

Not surprisingly, then, their godly example and consistency of life made a profound impression on their children. The children never caused a moment of trouble in the Christian school. As they graduated, several of the children went on to Christian colleges. Today, though none of them is in full-time Christian service, each is a faithful servant of Jesus Christ in his respective location. Mom and Dad had been examples "of the believer in word, in conversation, in charity, in spirit, in faith, in purity" (I Timothy 4:12). It paid off. When the harvest came later in life, their children revealed the spiritual character of their home, and their harvest will be everlasting.

* * *

Each element of training our children is important. There will be several more chapters toward that end, but folks, be aware. The genuineness of your Christian walk and spiritual character will have a profound impact on how your children develop spiritually. It works both ways. Where there is genuine godliness and spirituality in the lives of *both* parents, there likely will be a similar harvest in the children. However, if *one* parent is dragging his or her anchor spiritually and is living an inconsistent life spiritually, beware. The harvest likely will not be happy when it comes.

A major key in the matter of raising our children is that of genuine, day-to-day, godly living. There are not any short cuts or quick fixes. If you do not live the life according to the Book, the consequences will not be pleasant, and they will likely show up in your children. *"Be not deceived; God is not mocked: for whatsoever a man soweth, that shall he also reap"* (Galatians 6:7).

As I teach, preach, and counsel on this matter, some people get their hackles up. They bristle if the pastor comments about how their family deports itself. As far as they are concerned, "That ain't none of the pastor's business!" Then I think of how the Apostle Paul instructed young Timothy: *"in meekness instructing those that oppose themselves; if God peradventure will give them repentance to the acknowledging of the truth; And that they may recover themselves out of the snare of the devil, who are taken captive by him at his will"* (II Timothy 2:25-26).

People who are heading for trouble often react unkindly to a pastor trying to warn them of that trouble ahead. All the pastor can do is, in meekness, instruct these who are *opposing themselves* and tell them what affect this will have on their children. The scary thing is that they are playing with an adversary who can take their children captive spiritually. That ought to sober any Christian parent and turn them to consistent, godly living.

"Be not deceived; God is not mocked: for whatsoever a man (or woman) soweth, that shall he also reap. For he that soweth to his flesh shall of the flesh reap corruption; but he (or she) that soweth to the Spirit shall of the Spirit reap life everlasting." The issues of life are fundamentally spiritual. The issues of life include how our children turn out. The way we as parents live our lives spiritually will have a major impact upon the way our children turn out spiritually. For them to develop into godly, spiritual, disciplined, righteous, young adults will require that **both** of their parents present a consistent example of the same. It takes **both** parents pulling the load spiritually. Anything less is a spiritual tragedy in the making.

Chapter 9 - Fruit Inspecting

For Christians, the word "regenerated" has a theological sense. To be regenerated means to be born again. It is the "proof of the pudding." Only God knows the heart and only God knows whose names are recorded in the Book of Life in heaven. But Jesus said, *"Wherefore, by their fruits ye shall know them "* (Matthew 7:20).

There is a considerable number of people who profess salvation, but do not really possess it. Put another way, there are many people who claim to be saved who have never been born again. For if they had been born again, they would live their lives differently.

Being born again is more than just a theological concept. It is a reality. When a person is genuinely born again, they may not do all that they ought to do, nor may they be all they ought to be. However, if they have genuinely been born again, there will be a change in their lives. There will be a difference.

II Corinthians 5:17 says, *"Therefore, if any man be in Christ, he is a new creature: old things are passed away; behold, all things are become new."* It is noteworthy that this portion of Scripture does *not* say, "If any man be in Christ, he *ought* to be a new creature: old things *should* pass away, behold all things *should* become new." When a person is saved, he is at that instant born again; and if he is born again, there *will* be a difference.

I believe one problem in many Christian homes is that the children have made professions of faith, but have never actually been born again. Even more tragic is that they go on through life assuming that they are saved, when in fact they are not. Their lives frequently manifest the reality of their spiritual condition.

It is critically important that our children understand salvation. Nothing in life is more important. Their eternal destiny is at stake. As we seek to train them in the way that they should go, it will be considerably easier if they possess a new nature which after God has been *"created in righteousness and true holiness"* (Ephesians 4:24). A child who has a divinely created new nature within his or her heart will be spiritually sympathetic to being trained in righteousness. That new nature within has been so created by the Holy Spirit.

Therefore, it is of utmost importance that we carefully instruct and coach our children about salvation. Praise the Lord for godly Sunday School teachers and children's workers in the church. But parents should be the first to tell their children of the gospel of Jesus Christ.

Having been in the ministry for 25 years, I know that there are some wonderful, well-prepared, spiritually mature, and perceptive Sunday School teachers. I also know that some are weak, poorly prepared, and are not spiritually perceptive. Mom and Dad, you had best not rely on the Sunday School teacher to lay the foundation of salvation for your children. Hopefully, they can reenforce and amplify what you have taught at home. However, you need to be prepared to do the major teaching about salvation to your children.

Furthermore, you have the opportunity to spend far more time laying a foundation for the gospel. You simply have more time with your children than the weekly programs at the church.

Lack of Conviction

As a pastor, I have witnessed two major weaknesses in children's lives that relate to the matter of their salvation. The first matter is the conviction of sin. I am mindful of several individuals around the country who, through their growing up years, sat regularly in Sunday School and attended Christian schools. Their parents were faithful members of the church. These individuals sooner or later *professed* to be saved. Yet, today, they are sitting in a prison somewhere in the United States. They have essentially repudiated their salvation and make no pretense of being a Christian. They have broken their parents' hearts.

I think of an individual in a penitentiary in another state who could quote Scripture to make me ashamed. He professed to be saved. He had grown up in a Bible believing church. Yet today, he is serving a life sentence for multiple murders. I think of another individual who had grown up in a Christian home. Her parents had sacrificed to send her to a Christian school. When she was small, she always was in Sunday School and church. Today, she is serving time for a number of convictions. She too professed to be saved, but she has repudiated any relationship to Jesus Christ. I think of another individual whose parents were dedicated workers in the church. They saw to it that their children were always in church. They placed them in the Christian school. Despite those things, that fellow is serving time today.

For each one who is in a prison somewhere, I could tell about many others. Though they have not run afoul of the law, they are nevertheless living in deep sin. In some cases it is in sexual sin. In other cases it involves drugs. In other cases they have just given up on their Christian training and plunged head first into the world. They professed to be saved in their childhood; but in reality, they were never born again. They went through the motions and walked an aisle. They learned the language, but they were never regenerated.

(Paul wrote to Titus, *"They profess that they know God; but in works they deny him, being abominable, and disobedient, and unto every good work reprobate"* Titus 1:16. The context is of unsaved people, even though they have professed to know God.)

Once they had gone through the motions, sometimes even sincerely, there was never any more pressure on them to be saved. They were accepted by their peers in the church as having been born again. They may have even thought themselves to be born again. Therefore, as the years passed on, they conveniently hid behind that "experience" they had earlier in life. Except for the conviction of the Holy Spirit, no one ever bothered them again about getting saved. I was one such person.

As a boy of five, I had gone (or been taken) forward in an evangelistic meeting. I do not know who the preacher was. I do not remember what the sermon was about. In fact, as I recall, I slept through much of the service. I have absolutely no recollection of who prayed with me or how I was dealt with in the prayer room. In a later section, I will detail further the lack of spiritual understanding on my part that night. However, I have no recollection of praying a sinner's prayer. Though, evidently I did.

After that meeting, I was coached to tell others that I had gotten saved. Therefore, over the next fifteen years, if someone asked me if I was saved, I would reply, "Oh yes. I was saved when I was five years old."

Now, I believe that five-year-old children can be saved, but I do not believe that this pastor was saved when he was five. If it had not been for faithful parents who continued to pray for me over those years, I may not have been genuinely converted when I was in Bible college. I believe in my case and in many others, there was a lack of conviction about sin and its consequences in both heart and mind. It is a crucial prerequisite to the new birth.

Lack of Assurance

The second problem that frequently crops up in children concerning their salvation is a lack of assurance. Children make a profession of faith at some point in their lives. Later they question it. They frequently make multiple professions of faith trying to have assurance of their salvation. Only God knows the true spiritual condition of the heart. The fact that this is such a common experience in Bible-believing churches leads one to conclude that these children have not been led to clearly understand the matter of salvation.

There are several possible reasons for this. In some cases, children just do not remember much about their experience of making a profession of faith in Christ as Savior. They may have been young when they made a profession of faith. In other cases, they have never fully understood the matter of assurance of salvation and the fullness of it. Frequently, children will become convicted about some area of sin that has crept into their lives. Because they are under conviction about that sin, they come to the conclusion that they are not saved. There are a number of variations of that theme. In other cases because of immaturity, they are just confused. In still other cases, they are convicted because they really were not saved in the first place. The problem may have been a lack of genuine repentance and faith on their part. On the other hand, it may have stemmed from the fact that whoever counselled with them originally was not diligent in dealing with them.

Let me just add this word of caution before we go further. If your children come to you and indicate that they are not sure they are saved, take that very seriously. It may be they are just confused or do not fully understand the principle of the security of the believer. However, they may be genuinely convicted by the Holy Ghost of their need of salvation.

In Bible college, I was searching spiritually. I went to a spiritual leader and told him of my heart's confusion. He dismissed my concern and told me I was just seeking assurance of my salvation. Well, as it turned out, what I really was seeking was salvation. If that leader had been more sensitive, he may have been able to lead me to Christ on the spot.

If your children come to you and tell you they are not sure that they are saved, treat it as though they have never made any profession of faith. You do not know their hearts; only God does. Beware of saying "Oh, honey, you took care of that a long time ago. Don't you remember?" It may be that the Holy Ghost has been dealing in his heart. Do not assume that because he has otherwise gone through the motions that he is born again. If you do not know how to proceed, then perhaps a godly pastor can be of assistance to you. There are eternal stakes at risk.

Lack of Understanding

I believe that part of the problem lies in the fact that many Christians are fuzzy in their understanding of basic doctrine. The doctrine of salvation is one of them.

Let's look at some very basic Bible doctrine at this point. One of the fundamentals of New Testament Christianity is that an individual is saved by faith in Jesus Christ. You will find that the concept of salvation by faith in Christ appears in the New Testament over 200 times. One is saved by simple faith in Jesus

Christ as personal Savior. Nothing more. Nothing less. Over and over again, that principle is reiterated in the New Testament.

In Matthew 9:22 we read, *"And Jesus seeing their faith said, thy sins be forgiven thee."* In Luke 7:50 Jesus said, *"Thy faith hath saved thee; go in peace."* Again, in Luke 18:42 our Lord said, *"Thy faith hath saved thee."* In Romans 5:1 the Bible says, *"Therefore being justified by faith, we have peace with God through our Lord Jesus Christ."* In Ephesians 2:8-9 the Scripture says, *"For by grace are ye saved through faith."* And there are a multitude of other passages teaching that eternal life is by believing in Christ. No doubt, the most well known is John 3:16. *"For God so loved the world, that he gave his only begotten son, that whosoever believeth in him, should not perish, but have everlasting life."*

The English words "faith" and "believe" are translated from the same word in the Greek New Testament. (A similar situation exists in the Hebrew Old Testament.) Both words have the sense of "trust" in contemporary English. To believe in Jesus Christ (as in John 3:16) means to trust in Him. This is the very heart of New Testament teaching concerning salvation: to believe on or trust in Jesus Christ as one's personal Savior.

Lack of Faith

It may be helpful to understand that in our 20th century "American" English, there are a number of connotations to the word "faith" or "believe." Accordingly, there are several degrees of faith or belief. The first level of faith is *intellectual assent.* That is the concept of accepting something as historical fact. For example, I *believe* that George Washington was the first president of America. Or, I have *faith* in the statement that Abraham Lincoln was the author of the Gettysburg Address. These are legitimate uses of the word and concept of faith. But this is the lowest level of the concept of faith. In the realm of the spiritual, many people believe in God. They believe about Jesus Christ. They even believe all that the Bible describes concerning Jesus Christ. Unfortunately, the type of faith involved for them is this first level of faith.

They are only giving intellectual assent to the historical reality of God and of Jesus Christ. They believe in Christ in about the same fashion as they believe in George Washington. Both are historical figures and they, to that degree, believe in both.

Needless to say, this level of faith does not save any one. It is the kind of faith that James referred to when he said, *"the devils also believe and tremble"* (James 2:19). Satan and his minions know there is a God and, to that degree, they believe in God.

The second level of faith is *temporal faith.* People come to a crisis in their lives. It might be the crisis of a soldier in warfare. As the battle rages, the terrified soldier prays and asks God to spare his life. It might be a family member in a hospital waiting room praying and asking God to spare a loved one in surgery or in intensive care. It might be someone in some other storm of life asking God for help.

In each case, these individuals have prayed and, to some degree, have exercised faith in God. They have trusted Him for help in the crisis at hand. That is fine as far as it goes. God may honor their prayers and may even give them help. Yet this type of faith is not that saving faith that brings salvation. They have only trusted God for the need of the hour.

I have met people who think that because God delivered them from a car accident or from cancer or from a battle zone that they must be saved. I am afraid they may be in for a shock when they wake up in eternity.

The third level of faith is *saving faith.* This is the faith mentioned in the New Testament in relation to being saved. Though we will go into more detail later, saving faith is when a person realizes that he is lost and turns to and trusts in Jesus Christ as his only salvation.

Lack of Repentance

If we go through the New Testament, we find that another concept is intermingled with the concept of saving faith. In fact, it sometimes is used synonymously with the word faith. That concept is of repentance. For example in Acts 3:19, Peter said, *"Repent ye therefore and be converted . . . ."* In Acts 11:18 the early church rejoiced to hear of the salvation of Cornelius's household. *"When they heard these things, they held their peace, and glorified God saying, Then hath God also to the Gentiles granted repentance unto life."*

Paul described to the leadership of the Ephesian church how his ministry had been in *"Testifying both to the Jews and also to the Greeks, repentance toward God, and faith toward our Lord Jesus Christ"* (Acts 20:21). In II Corinthians 7:10 Paul wrote to the Corinthian church that *"godly sorrow worketh repentance to salvation . . . ."*

Now, let us make it clear that salvation is not faith plus repentance. But rather, saving faith includes repentance. Repentance is not doing anything. It is not a deed, act, work, or rite. Rather, it is a change of the direction of one's heart. It basically means an attitude of the heart in turning from sin and self and turning to God. That's what Paul was referring to in Acts 20:21 when he referred to *"repentance toward God and faith in our Lord Jesus Christ."*

Saving faith is the human heart turning to God and then trusting in Jesus Christ. It is like the two sides of one coin. On the one side is the matter of a turning of the heart to God and on the other side is the matter of trusting in Jesus Christ. In reality, it is one spiritual step of turning to and trusting in Jesus Christ.

Trusting in Christ as personal Savior implies a realization of one's spiritual condition before God. The Bible clearly teaches that we all are sinners (Romans 3:23). Our sinfulness is due to the sinful nature we were born with. It also is a result of a lifetime of willfully violating God's moral and spiritual law.

Therefore, each of us is a sinner by nature and by volition. Moreover, the Bible teaches very clearly that a Holy God will judge and condemn both sin and sinners. In a nutshell, that is what it means in Romans 6:23 *"the wages of sin is death."* Sin ultimately will condemn a person to an eternal hell, which is also known as the second death (Revelation 20:14). In short, this is what the Bible refers to as being lost.

Now, it is important that children understand the fix they are in spiritually. They need to have some understanding of the fact that the Bible says they are lost. The terminology is not critical, but the concept is.

There is no need to seek the Savior if there is no understanding of one's lost condition. For children to be able to trust Jesus Christ they need to realize that they are lost. They may not understand all the ramifications and implications of that fact but they do need to realize that without Jesus Christ they are in big trouble.

Then, and only then, is an individual ready to trust in God's only hope of salvation—the resurrected Christ. Even as there is the part of trusting Christ, there is also the part of turning to Him. That may seem inconsequential, but I believe that here is a spiritual reason why some go through the motions of believing in Christ but are not really born again.

They seemingly want the fire escape but there is no interest in turning to God. There is no interest in repentance. They have the attitude, "God, gimme salvation, but I'm gonna keep on doing my own thing." Now, not everyone's attitude may be as crass as that. However, if there is no real turning to God from the heart, they have missed the prerequisite for actually trusting Christ. I believe this is one major reason why many who profess Christ never truly possess the new birth.

Therefore, saving faith is a melding together of a number of basic spiritual truths.

1. Realize that you are lost and face judgment.
2. Willingly turn to the God whom you have sinned against.
3. Trust in Jesus Christ as your personal Savior.

It is not necessary for one to articulate all these finer theological points and understand all the ramifications of salvation. There must be, however, some basic understanding of need, and there must be a willingness to turn to and trust in Jesus Christ. Praise the Lord, salvation can be obtained through as simple a prayer as, "Lord, be merciful to me a sinner."

Obviously, children are not going to understand all the theological implications of salvation and all about the work of Christ. Children, if properly taught, can fully trust Christ as their personal Savior and be saved. The minimum age will vary depending upon how much exposure to the gospel they have had and how well they have been taught by their parents.

Lack of Bible Basics

There are two irreducible minimums necessary for children to get saved. (The fact is, this is the same for any age. There is only one plan of salvation, and it is the same for children as well as for adults.) Those two irreducible minimums are:

(1) **A clear realization of one's lost condition**. The terminology is not what is critical. Whether it is conveyed in the word hell or being lost or perishing, the conviction of going to hell or of being lost is absolutely critical. That is what a person is going to be saved from.

(2) **A clear realization that only Jesus Christ can save him.**
The two words in the title to the old hymn "Jesus Saves" convey
a profound spiritual truth. Children may not understand all the
implications of saving faith and all that Christ has done for them.
However, they must have a tacit realization of *who* Jesus Christ
is and that *He* is able to save them. When a child understands:
(1) his lost condition and (2) that Jesus Christ can save him from
that condition, he is basically ready to be saved.

Now, there must be the *willingness* to turn to Christ. This is
the ingredient of repentance.

As a young man in my junior year at Pillsbury Baptist Bible
College, God convicted me. I had never really been saved though
I had been a *professing* Christian for the preceding 15 years. On
the Thursday before Thanksgiving in 1966, I sat in my assigned
seat in the daily Pillsbury chapel service. I do not remember who
the speaker was that day, and I do not remember what the chapel
message was about. After chapel I returned to my dormitory
room because I had a free hour.

As I lay on my bed, alone in my room, a still small voice in
my heart asked me, "Dave, if you died today, what would happen
to you?" In my mind I thought, "Well, I'd go to heaven because
I am a Christian." Then the Spirit said, "When did you become
a Christian?" I thought, "When I was five years old." The Holy
Spirit said, "What happened then?" I thought, "I went forward in
a church service." Then the Holy Spirit said, "Well, then what
happened?" All of a sudden it became very fuzzy. I could not
remember what happened.

By this point in my college education, I had received some
theological training. I knew that a person needed to understand
that he was a sinner and on his way to hell. As I thought back,
I honestly had no recollection then of the fact of my sinfulness.
I tried to remember if I had any conviction of the fact that I was
on my way to an eternal hell. Again, up came a blank. I did not
remember actually praying and asking Jesus Christ to save me.

I very well may have done that, but I had no recollection of it. The thing that began to disturb me was that I really had no recollection of any conviction when I was a boy of five. I think a five-year-old can comprehend that to some degree but I had no recollection of it.

Then, I began to think back over my life to that point. I knew that the Bible taught that *"if any man be in Christ, he is a new creature"* (II Corinthians 5:17). I knew that if a person was really saved, there would be an interest in the things of God. There would be some sort of internal aversion to sin. Anyone who knew me during my teenage years would have remembered me as a rebellious preacher's kid.

I had absolutely no interest in the things of God. I only went to church because my dad was the pastor, and I had to go. I could not have cared less about the Bible. Things like witnessing and having a testimony were about as alien to me as living in Afghanistan.

I loved the world and the things that were in the world. My mind and my vocabulary were as foul as any one else in the world. I thought like the world thought. I liked what the world did, and I wanted to do what the world did. Only the strictness of my upbringing and of the college I was attending prevented me from actually doing a significant amount of it.

I lay there on my bed that morning in November 1966. As I mulled all of this over in my mind, I knew that I had no recollection of conviction when I went forward as a boy. I reflected over the fact that there had never been any change in my life spiritually that I could remember. I knew the sinfulness of my heart as a 20-year-old college student, and I considered the lack of interest in the things of God in my life.

Slowly that November morning, the Holy Spirit convicted me of the fact that I had never really been saved. I had gone through the motions of it as a small boy and had professed salvation all those years. For the first time in my life it was dawning on me that I was not saved, and for someone who had assumed to be saved for the past 15 years, it came as quite some shock.

So, I lay there and struggled with the whole matter. The Holy Spirit continued to place thoughts into my mind. As I thought about the situation, it suddenly dawned upon me, "If I am not saved, then I am on my way to hell." I had never in my entire life given any serious consideration to that fact. It kind of shook me up. Then I foolishly thought, "Well, everyone thinks that I am a Christian. I'll just keep faking it." However, the Holy Spirit said something like, "Go ahead and fake it, Dave, but when you die it will be *your* funeral. Nobody else's."

I realized that I was dealing with a serious matter. After wrestling spiritually with the conviction of the Holy Spirit for some time, I knew I had to settle the matter. I knelt beside my bed and prayed, "Dear Lord, I know I am a sinner. I really don't know what happened when I was five years old. But I don't think I really was saved then. Oh Lord, please save me and cleanse me of my sin and give me eternal life."

There were no bolts of lightning or thunder claps, but a peace swept across my heart. I knew I had settled the matter. There no longer was any doubt. I had trusted Christ and I knew it. I claimed Romans 10:13, *"For whosoever shall call upon the name of the Lord, shall be saved."* This time there had been a clear understanding of my lost condition, and this time there was a deep willingness to turn to Christ and trust Him. Praise the Lord, He saved me.

Very soon thereafter, my life began to make some radical changes. Even as a student in a Christian college, my interest in serving the Lord had been somewhere between little and none. Witnessing and soul winning were as alien to me as some foreign language. Not only did I not know how; I did not care.

Now I suddenly became burdened for the guy I worked with at a TV repair shop in town.

Within six weeks of making peace with Jesus Christ, I had led him to Christ and attempted to win my other co-worker there. I began going to a reformatory to help conduct services and then on to the Minnesota State Penitentiary at Stillwater, Minnesota, for services. Before long I was preaching at the prison myself. Prior to my salvation experience, I honestly could not have cared less about such things. Something had happened to me. I had been born again.

As I have reflected back on the experience I had as a boy, several things have become clear. Some concerned individual had encouraged me to go forward in that service. But I did not have any conviction of the fact that I was lost. Again, the terminology was not the critical concept. I just did not grasp it.

I think children of that age can grasp the gospel. It was just that particular night I was not convicted of it. Because there was no conviction of my lost condition, there was no real turning to nor trusting in the Savior that night. It is important that a child grasp his spiritual need.

When our Heather was of about kindergarten age, little by little she came to understand in her mind about salvation. She had heard us teach at length about why she needed to be saved and how to be saved. However, when push came to shove, she did not *want* to get saved. Thankfully, not too long after that, she came to a point where she was *willing* to turn her little heart over to the Lord and trust Him. She did, and we praise the Lord for that.

Created Confusion

Perhaps one reason some children go through confusion is the vague terminology sometimes used. They may lack assurance, or they may not be genuinely saved at all. It seems we have a tendency to use theological euphemisms to explain the gospel.

They sound nice and appropriate for use with a child. Unfortunately, some are not well grounded in biblical facts.

For example the little phrase of, "Ask Jesus to come into your heart" sounds very nice. It seems so appropriate for use with a primary age child. It gives a kind of warm and fuzzy sound to the more austere theological language found in the Bible. There is only one problem. Nowhere in the Bible is the concept directly taught that asking Jesus into one's heart is the basis of personal salvation.

Now, some might argue that John 1:12 could be so paraphrased where we read, *"But as many as received him, to them gave he power to become the sons of God . . . ."* And indeed receiving Christ might be so paraphrased as to mean asking him into our heart. However, I believe in a matter so crucial as one's salvation, it is very risky to begin substituting our words for God's words. At the very least, use of such euphemisms lends itself to questioning the assurance of salvation. Here is why.

The bedrock of assurance of our salvation is the ability to go to the Word of God and remind one's self that once upon a time I did exactly what this verse said to do. For example, "I called upon the name of the Lord and asked him to save me just like it says in Romans 10:13." Or "On such and such a date, I believed in Jesus Christ just like it says to do in John 3:16," etc. If we can help a child to directly link his profession of Christ to Scripture, we will have helped him immensely in overcoming doubts about his salvation. He can always return to the Word of God to allay confusion and doubts.

A similar argument might be made about Revelation 3:20 where Jesus said to the church at Laodicea, *"Behold, I stand at the door and knock: If any man hear my voice, and open the door, I will come in to him, and will sup with him, and he with me."* First of all, in the context, it is not clear if the Lord is even referring directly to salvation here. The context lends itself to the thought that He was excluded from the church at Laodicea.

They were so wrapped up with their prosperity and programs that they had forgotten the Lord. He, in effect, was on the outside of the church knocking to come in. Now to be sure, there likely is a secondary application or illustration of salvation. Nevertheless, we need to be very careful about building a foundation for our children's salvation upon a secondary application of a portion of Scripture.

I am not suggesting that using a phrase such as, "Asking Jesus to come into your heart," is insufficient cause for the Lord to save a child with an open heart. There no doubt are many who have been sweetly converted to Christ by asking Him to come into their hearts.

The point is, that approach to salvation is not directly anchored in Scripture. It is anchored in an *interpretation* of Scripture. If a person is genuinely saved by "asking Jesus into his heart," it is because in his heart he in fact turned to Jesus and trusted Him as personal Savior.

Why not use more direct Scriptural language in presenting Christ to our children? I believe it will help alleviate some of the confusion that so many children go through later in doubting their salvation.

At the least, such theological euphemisms can create confusion and doubt later in life. At the worst, they may obscure the truth to such a degree that a child does not genuinely trust Jesus Christ. The tragic consequences of that are obvious. The bottom line is that these children, though they went through the motions of accepting Christ, never really were born again. The implications of that are serious.

Other euphemisms that are sometimes used are: "making a commitment to Christ," or "making a decision for Christ." It may surprise you to know that the phrase "accepting Christ," per se, does not appear in the Bible. If the truths of the need of salvation and of the ability of Christ to save are clearly taught, then such phrases may not be harmful. The greater principle at this point, however, is of trying to use terms and phrases that are directly from Scripture.

Why presume to improve upon the basic terminology and phrasing of the Word of God? Moreover, why not use terminology that can be directly related to in the Bible. At some later time when assurance is needed or when doubts arise about salvation, they can always return to the specific Scripture used when they were saved. It should behoove us to be careful in explaining the gospel to our children. The spiritual foundation of their lives is being laid. Any builder knows that a foundation not properly laid will cause much trouble later. Stay as close to the scriptural terms and phrases as possible. If you feel you must use theological euphemisms, then make sure that they are secondary and used for illustration. Stick to the Book for the primary terms.

Explaining Salvation to Children

Let me share several suggestions concerning explaining salvation to children.

1. **Begin early in life**. A pre-school child very well may be too young to receive Christ as personal Savior. But that should not prevent you from explaining all about it. When our children were small, they learned about Jesus. They heard about salvation and heaven and hell. They were taught about hell, not only from a theological point of view, but also that they would go there some day if they did not get saved. That may seem heavy for a preschool age child, but it was the truth. As the children approached their school years, each of them, on her own and in her own unique way trusted Christ as her personal Savior.

When is a child old enough to get saved? That will vary not only with the spiritual background the child has, but it will also vary within a given family. It is almost trite to say that all children are different, but it is true. The crucial point is when a child is old enough to understand the necessary truths. Children need to understand that they are lost sinners and that Jesus Christ can save them if they will only trust Him. Once that point arrives, it is time to get serious about leading our children to Christ.

2. **Clearly define terms**. To understand the gospel a person must understand basic scriptural terms. Explain who Jesus Christ is. Explain not only the various stories about our Lord's life and ministry that are so common for children, but also explain His person. Explain that He is God's Son. Explain that He is a part of the Godhead. Explain what happened on Calvary and how our sin was placed upon Him as He suffered and died. Explain how He died paying for our sin. And by all means explain how He arose and is alive today.

It is very important that children have a grasp of the concept of sin. Until they understand sin and that they are sinners, they probably are not ready to get saved. Children, like adults, need to understand the guilt of their sin and its consequences before they can turn to and trust the Savior.

Over the years as children would come forward at an invitation to receive Christ, we have always taught our workers to carefully question the child about sin. Frequently, when children are asked if they have sinned, they will answer, "no." The worker then would proceed to explain that sin is when we do wrong. The worker might then ask the child, "Do you ever do wrong?" If the child says, "no" again, he probably does not have the understanding to go further with the plan of salvation. Equating sin with wrongdoing is a simple way to illustrate what sin is. It is not until a child can relate to the cry of the publican, *"God, be merciful to me a sinner . . ."* (Luke 18:13) that he or she is near salvation.

Hell is another concept that small children may have trouble understanding. When our daughter Heather was still in her preschool years, we went over and over again how that hell was a place of fire and that bad people went there forever because of their sin. It did not ring a bell with her. So we tried to illustrate that it was sort of like going to jail. Bad people went to jail because they did bad things.

In the town of Pekin, Illinois, where we lived at the time, the county jail was on one of the main streets in the downtown area. While passing it on several occasions, I pointed out to her that there was the jail. But her little mind could not quite distinguish between hell and jail.

At about that same time, I was ministering to a man connected with our church. He wound up in jail for violating a court restraining order in a marriage separation. I would go to the jail to visit this fellow several times a week. One day, I came home and mentioned that I had gone to the jail. Little Heather's eyes got wide with astonishment. She said, "Well, how did you get out?" She still had not quite figured out the difference between jail and hell. Not too long thereafter, it all came into focus in her mind. She realized her lost condition and sweetly called upon Jesus to save her.

Be so careful to explain and define the crucial terms of salvation. If you must use "euphemisms" make sure that they are rooted in the clear statement of Scripture. In fact, use the Bible and let the children see and read the portions of the gospel itself, *"for it is the power of God unto salvation"* (Romans 1:16).

3. **Family devotions and bed time are ideal forums**. In an earlier chapter, we covered in some detail the matter of family devotions (page 129 and following). Suffice it to say at this point, though, that family devotions or the family altar is an excellent forum for teaching our children about salvation. In the years when our children were small, we would frequently go over the basics of salvation in our family devotions.

I am sure that some will protest that I am a pastor and have had special training. That no doubt has been a help. But explaining salvation should be fairly basic to any born-again Christian. It may require some forethought to avoid cliches and euphemisms that may only cloud the picture. But as an adult, born-again Christian, you should be able to explain the basics concerning salvation such as: What is sin? What will happen to sinners? Who is Jesus Christ, and what did He do on the cross? How may a person receive Christ and trust Him?

Another similar forum is bed time when many a Christian parent will kneel to pray with their children before they go to bed. That is a practice to be encouraged. If that is already in place, it is a simple thing in addition to praying, to talk about the gospel with our children. Do not push or pressure. Just teach them all about it. As they get older and understand more, the Holy Spirit will convict their hearts. One day, they will be tender and ready to receive Christ if you have laid the ground work and prepared their hearts and minds. I can think of no one I would rather lead to Christ than my own children. In our home, we had the privilege of witnessing both of our children receive Jesus Christ as their personal Savior.

In summary, I believe that we as parents need to be the primary teachers of our children concerning salvation. We need to be careful to clearly define our terminology. Avoid little phrases that might sound nice for a child, but may be vague or not have direct scriptural basis. Make sure they are clear on the irreducible minimums of understanding—a realization that they are lost and the sufficiency of Jesus Christ to save if they will trust Him. If you are not sure of basic Bible doctrine concerning salvation, bone up on it. It will be good for your sake, and it will be most helpful in teaching your children.

Chapter 10 - The Battle Is On

The material in this chapter will pertain to more than the training of our children. Nevertheless, it will pertain directly to godliness. I speak of the spiritual dichotomy of the old nature and the new.

We all were born with a human nature that is spiritually depraved, spiritually fallen, and naturally sinful. **All** of the sin that ever will be in our lives comes through the old nature the Bible calls the flesh. This is that old, depraved, fallen, sinful nature. Your cute little boy or girl running around your house has a depraved, inherently sinful, human nature. Again, the common term in the New Testament for this nature is "the flesh."

In Galatians 5:19-21, the Apostle Paul sets forth a partial list of the works (or the spiritual products) of the flesh. It is an ugly specter. Notice that the list begins with sexual sin: adultery, fornication, uncleanness, and lasciviousness. The latter two refer to the broader area of sexual impurity including, but not limited to, pornography, dirty jokes, and various forms of lewd sexual arousal. Earlier, we have recounted some of the sad stories of young people from Christian homes who have gotten into sexual sin. Remember that such behavior is a direct result or work of the flesh . . . the old sinful nature.

The list continues: "idolatry and witchcraft." Young people today idolize rock performers, entertainers, and professional athletes. Might that not be construed as a form of idolatry? Could this possibly be a modern day application of the second commandment wherein God said: *"Thou shalt not make unto thee any graven image, or any likeness of any thing that is in heaven above, or that is in the earth beneath, or that is in the water under the earth"* (Exodus 20:4)?

Have you ever taken a look at the posters idolizing rock stars, entertainers, and athletes? Could it be that our young people are guilty of idolatry? If so, it is a product of the old nature.

Also, what about witchcraft with the prevalence of the occult. Whether it be games, such as Dungeons and Dragons, or Ouija boards, they are occultic. Did you know that the word translated as "witchcraft" in the Greek New Testament is *"pharmacia"*? That Greek word is strikingly similar to the familiar English word "pharmacy." It has to do with the illicit drug usage which was common in occultic practices in ancient times. In any event, the Bible teaches that such activities emanate from the flesh, the old nature.

The list in Galatians 5 goes on with "hatred and variance" which refers to an argumentative, uncooperative attitude. "Emulations" which means bitterness is followed by "wrath" which is the loosing of one's temper. "Strife" means bickering and fighting. "Seditions" means divisive, and "heresy" literally means being opinionated and bullheaded. All of these emanate from the flesh and are evident in the lives of children and teens.

How about "envying"? Have you ever seen a child envious or jealous of another? It likewise is from the flesh, as is "murder." Finally, Paul includes "drunkenness and revelings." I am sure drunkenness needs no further explanation. "Revelings" is a reference to wild partying. More than one Christian teenager has been guilty of that.

Now the truth is, young people from Christian families across the land wind up doing some or all of these things. I have recounted numerous true stories throughout this book of young people from Christian homes who have "gone off the deep end" into sin of one sort or another. However, they **all** had one thing in common. **They** **all** **were walking in the flesh.**

The New Nature

When an individual is born again, God creates within him a new nature. Ephesians 4:24 speaks of our new nature as being created in righteousness and true holiness. Only the new nature will produce righteous and holy activity. Sin *never* emanates from the new nature. It is pure. It is that portion of our human personality that will go to heaven when we die. It is that portion of us spiritually that has been regenerated or quickened.

Therefore, if young people can be so directed and trained to live their life predominantly in the new nature, they, for the most part, are going to win the battle over temptation and sin. That is what Paul meant in Galatians 5:16 where he said, *"Walk in the Spirit, and ye shall not fulfill the lust of the flesh."*

Let me digress for a moment to clarify a point. I think this may help us understand Galatians 5. Throughout Galatians 5, the translators of the English Bible have consistently used a capital letter to begin the word "Spirit." This, of course, implies the Holy Spirit, but exactly how does one walk in the Holy Spirit?

In the Greek manuscripts, no distinction was made between

upper case and lower case letters. The introduction of capital letters in our English Bible is actually interpretive on the part of the translators and is not inspired as such. I say all of that to say this. The word "spirit" could just as well have been translated with a lower case "s".

I am of the opinion that using the word "spirit" and applying it to our new nature in Galatians 5 makes more sense and is more consistent with the context. For throughout the latter portion of the chapter, Paul seems to be clearly contrasting the old nature with the new nature. Therefore, it is my understanding in Galatians 5 that when the Apostle Paul refers to the "Spirit" it rather is a reference to our new nature in Christ (our new spirit). (The point may be moot when we realize that our new spirit has been born of the Holy Spirit and thus created by God.) Nevertheless, when Paul says to "walk in the spirit," I believe he is referring to our new spiritual nature rather than the Holy Spirit.

Walking in the Spirit

As born-again Christians, we indeed do have two spiritual natures. Yet, God has created us as spiritually monophonic. Therefore, we can only live (or walk) in one or the other at any given time. We can either live in the flesh or in the spirit (the new nature). Therefore, if we can so train our children to walk in the spirit (the new nature) as the basic operation of their Christian life, the battle will be won. No sin ever comes through the new nature.

Actually, most of the teaching of the Word of God concerning the Christian life focuses toward that end. Likewise, there ought to be a major goal of godliness for our children. Train your children to walk in the spirit (i.e., the new nature). Before long, we will get to practical advice on that matter.

Continuing further in the chapter, the Apostle contrasts the product of the flesh with the product of the new nature. The old nature brings forth all manner of corruption and evil, but notice the fruit of the new nature in Galatians 5:22-23. As one is born again and actually begins to *grow* in the grace and knowledge of our Lord Jesus Christ, a lovely cluster of fruit begins to develop in that life. This cluster of fruit includes love, joy, peace, longsuffering, gentleness, goodness, faith, meekness and temperance among others.

If our young people develop such spiritual character traits, what a difference it will make in their lives. Contrast this to if they are allowed to develop the corrupt works of the flesh. *Unless and until we train our children to walk in the spirit rather than the flesh, we are only dealing with symptoms and never getting to the root of the matter.*

As Paul said in Galatians 5:25, *"If we live in the Spirit, let us also walk in the Spirit."* I understand that to mean, if we are alive in the new nature, then we will actually live in it. The problem in legions of Christian young people is that they may possess a new nature, but they are not living in it. There is only one alternative way for them to live . . . in the flesh. When Christian young people live in the flesh, they are capable of doing any of the things listed in the works of the flesh of Galatians 5. And that is exactly why so many Christian young people have a problem with sin.

If the adversary, the devil, can urge Christian young people to live in the flesh, then he can tempt them virtually at will. Have no question about it. Satan will target the young people of Christian parents. He walks about as a roaring lion seeking whom he may devour. Children of Christian parents do not have to be unduly vulnerable to his attack, but often they are. The problem is that of Christian parents who do not equip and so train their children to walk in the spirit.

The Way the Flesh Works

Next, we will consider the way the flesh works. In Galatians 5:24 Paul goes on to speak of the flesh and its *affections and lusts*. The word "affections" in the Greek refers essentially to our feelings. The word "lust" is used regularly throughout the New Testament in connection with the flesh.

In our late 20th Century vernacular, the word "lust" usually denotes sexual lust, and that is *one* sense of the word. But its scope is far broader than that. In the Greek New Testament, the word used for "lust" basically means "desires." Our old nature operates on the wavelength of desires, likes, wants, and feelings. Therefore, a young person who is walking in the flesh will live on the basis of what he or she *wants*, or *likes*, or *feels like*.

Witness this scene. Little Johnny comes home from school and his mother says, "Son, go do your homework." Johnny promptly replies, "But, Mom, I do not *want* to." Or perhaps, "Awe, Mom, I don't *feel like it.*" How many parents have ever heard that? Do you know what the root problem is here? At this particular moment, little Johnny is living in the flesh. He is making decisions based upon what he *wants* or *feels like*.

Now, imagine this scene. Big Johnny is out with his buddies, and they offer him a beer. "Hey, Johnny, this is cool stuff. It will make you *feel* good." And because Johnny does not *want* to be a nerd to his buddies, he gets drunk for the first time. Rather than doing what was right, he succumbed to the pressure of *wanting* to be accepted by his buddies (peer pressure).

We could look at many different scenarios. Little Billy *does not want* to read his Bible, so he does not. Susie *does not feel like* going to church, so she does not. Chucky *likes* the video game at the store, so he shoplifts it. Teenage Jane *wants* attention from the boys, so she dresses provocatively. Bill and Kim *feel* like going all the way, so they do. Missy *wants* to look cool, so she takes up smoking. Michael *likes* the arousal from pornography, so he secretly looks at it. Debbie *likes* rock music, so she listens to it. Bud *does not feel like* getting up on time, so he does not. Sheila *feels like* pouting, so she does. Brad *likes* his bad attitude, so he wears it.

Now, notice in every one of these potential scenes, decisions were made on the basis of *want, like, or feelings.* Whether the deed or attitude was right was not considered. Whether they ought or ought not to have done . . . whatever, was irrelevant. "Who cares! This is what *I want* to do."

The problem here is fundamentally spiritual. In each and every one of these hypothetical situations, the subject was manifesting the symptoms of living in the flesh. They were doing what they *wanted* to do. And that is how the flesh operates. Its basic *modus operandi* is its affections *(feelings)* and lusts *(wants and desires).* The truth is, many adults live the same way. And one reason that children and teenagers in Christian homes live that way is because their parents' habits of living are similar. Such shallow and selfish living is systemic to the flesh. People operating in the flesh live that way, but the results of such living are found in that ugly list in Galatians 5.

Ephesians 4:22-24 goes right to the heart of the matter. The Apostle wrote, *"That ye put off concerning the former conversation the old man, which is corrupt according to the deceitful lusts; and be renewed in the spirit of your mind; And that ye put on the new man, which after God is created in righteousness and true holiness."*

Briefly, that phrase "former conversation" is a reference to the old way of living in the flesh. Moreover, Paul warns us that the "old man" (the flesh) is corrupt according to its deceitful lusts. It appeals to our desires. It implies that if we satisfy our desires, we will be satisfied and happy.

Ironically, the indulging in the desires of our old nature brings only brief and illusory gratification. The long term results are corrupt. They emanate from a spiritual nature that is corrupt.

Moreover, those who live their lives pursuing and satisfying their desires and feelings inevitably are miserable and unhappy. The whole spectrum and results of the old nature are corrupt. Then notice again in Ephesians 4:23, we are to be renewed in the spirit of our mind. One might ask, "What does that mean?" The answer is in verse 24. *"Put on the new man which after God is created in righteousness and true holiness."* If we have been born again, we have a new nature.

The Spirit in Action

Notice how this nature is described. It has been created in *righteousness and true holiness*. That is, our new man (the spirit of our mind) has been created righteous. It has been created holy. When we then actually live (or walk) in that new nature, righteousness and holiness become the controlling characteristics in our life. *A person walking in the spirit (the new man) will make decisions based upon whether something is right or pleasing to God.*

For one walking in the spirit, the very basis of decision making is fundamentally different. Those living in the flesh will look at something on the basis of whether they want to or feel like it. One walking in the spirit will make decisions based upon, is it right?

Johnny, as a born again Christian, is tempted to cheat on a test. He assumes that he can get away with it, and he thinks it will help his grade. But immediately, he reconsiders because it is not *right*. In all likelihood, that decision was prompted by the new nature within him.

Vicki, as a Christian teenager, has deep feelings about her boy friend. The urge and opportunity are present for sexual intimacy. But at the same moment she reminds herself, *"It is not right."* And she quickly backs off. The new nature created in righteousness and true holiness has dictated her actions.

Don does not really feel like getting up that extra 15 minutes early to spend some time in the Word and prayer. But the new nature within him quickly reminds him that he *ought* to get up and spend some time with the Lord. The new man within him has constrained him to do what is right.

Sue, as a teenage Christian, does not really want to tithe on her part-time income. But she does because it is right.

The new nature is doing what is right. Hence, a Christian living in the new nature (walking in the spirit) will be strongly influenced to do right at any given decision.

How to Walk in the Spirit

Now, how can we train our children to walk in the spirit and not in the flesh? What follows is a summary of what has gone before in this book.

1. **The first and most obvious step is to insure that our children have a new nature**. It is called being born again. It is the basic salvation experience. If you are fuzzy on the matter, go back to the chapter that goes into considerable detail on the subject of salvation. Only by receiving Jesus Christ as personal Savior may one have a new nature to walk in. Furthermore, as a parent, you will find it difficult, if not impossible to lead your children any farther spiritually than you have gone yourself.

2. **The strength of the new nature is in the Word of God and the things of God**. Therefore, it is incumbent upon us as parents to see that our children are daily in the Word of God. There is effectively no way a Christian can walk in the new nature if they are not regularly in the Word of God. It is the spiritual milk, bread, meat and water necessary for the sustenance and strength of the new nature.

If your children are not in the Word of God every single day, they will walk in the flesh. Period! We just come back to spiritual basics. God's Word is absolutely essential to living in the new nature. There never will be the spiritual strength or impetus to walk in the spirit apart from the Word of God. *"Thy word have I hid in mine heart that I might not sin against thee"* (Psalm 119:11). *"Wherewithal shall a young man cleanse his way? By taking heed thereto according to thy word"* (Psalm 119:9). Additionally, the other associated things of God such as prayer and faithfulness to the things of God only strengthen and renew our spiritual nature.

This all reminds me of an illustration I heard my father use over the years in his preaching.

A missionary working with native American peoples had led an Indian man to Christ. He had worked with this fellow and helped him get grounded in his Christian life. Some time later he again paid a visit to this native Christian.

The missionary asked the Indian how he was doing in his Christian life. The Indian replied, "Indian have big battle on inside. It like bad dog and good dog. Bad dog always fighting with good dog. Good dog try to do right, but bad dog always try to do wrong." The missionary replied, "Which dog wins?" "Dog Indian feed most," came the answer.

Unless we daily feed the new man, the old man likely will get the victory. Get your children into the Word and keep them in it.

3. **Carefully lay the foundation of righteousness in the lives of your children.** The new man, by its very nature, is righteous. We as parents need to constantly reenforce that fact with the principle of righteousness in the minds of our children. It will pave the way for them to do what is right. Teaching the principle of righteousness over and over again will prepare the way for our children to merge into living in the spirit.

Righteousness and the new nature fit together hand and glove. The new nature has been cut out of the same cloth as righteousness. Stress and emphasize it continually in your home.

Needless to say, set an example of it. Doing such will reenforce the principle of righteousness for your children.

4. **Insist upon a disciplined life.** The very concept of self-discipline is antithetical to the flesh. The old nature schmoozes along doing what it wants to do, and avoiding doing what it does not feel like doing. Self-discipline forces us to do what we ought to do. That is very close, if not identical, to doing what is right.

It should be pointed out that the old nature will automatically come on line if nothing is done about it. (That is another reason for going to the Lord in prayer and the Word the first thing each day.) If I do absolutely nothing spiritually each day concerning the flesh versus the spirit, I will automatically be in the flesh.

When I turn on the computer, it automatically "wakes up" with a basic menu on the screen and with the basic Disk Operating System (DOS) in operation. If I would shift it to a higher operating system (Windows) and specific word processing software, I must take specific steps or the computer will remain in its initial mode.

So it is with the flesh and the spirit. Unless and until I take specific steps to rise up out of the flesh and walk in the spirit, I will remain in the flesh. This is one reason why so many Christian young people wind up in all the corruption of the flesh, especially in their teenage years. They have never been trained and disciplined to deal with the flesh and put on the new man each day.

5. **Train your children to put off the old nature and put on the new man each day.** Notice how the Scripture uses the analogy of changing clothes. In Ephesians 4:22 and 24 Paul talks about putting off the old man and putting on the new man. Most people each day take off their dirty clothes and put on clean clothes. It is basic the world over. If I take no action on the matter, I soon will not smell too good. I must initiate action to put off the unclean and put on the clean. It is a daily ritual. In fact, when the temperatures are hot and I have been working out

in the weather, I may put on clean clothes more than once a day. In reality, we often need to deal with the flesh more than once a day. Unfortunately, the old nature has a way of sneaking back into the foreground of our lives more than we care to admit.

6. **A corollary in the New Testament is of crucifying our flesh.** In Galatians 5:24 the Apostle wrote, *"And they that are Christ's have crucified the flesh with the affections and lusts."* Without going into the technicalities of the Greek, the verb tense could be translated as, *"And they that are Christ's crucify the flesh . . . ."* In other words, God's people ought to deal with the flesh as often as necessary.

Romans 6:6 says, *"Knowing this, that our old man is crucified with him . . . ."* Then in Romans 6:11 we read, *"Likewise reckon ye also yourselves to be dead indeed unto sin, but alive unto God through Jesus Christ our Lord."* The word "reckon" essentially means to make up our mind. Hence, to reckon ourselves to be dead to sin means to make up our minds, that as far as we are concerned, sin is dead in our lives today.

Jesus said, *"If any man will come after me, let him deny himself, and take up his cross daily, and follow me."* There is probably more implied here than just the matter of the flesh. But notice the sequence our Lord set forth. (1) *Deny ourselves* (which very well may be a reference to disciplining ourselves to do as we ought rather than what we want). (2) *Take up our cross daily.* Might this not be a reference to crucifying the flesh? I think so. (3) *Follow me.* A disciple is one who has disciplined himself to follow Jesus Christ. Evidently, we will never fully follow Jesus Christ while we give allowance to the old nature.

Each day, we must deal with our flesh. Reckon it to be dead. Crucify it. And crucify it as often as is necessary. Parents, we need to teach our children to do the same.

7. **Pray and ask the assistance of the Holy Spirit.** Each day as I meet the Lord in prayer in the morning, I pray and also ask the Holy Spirit to help me to crucify my flesh. He is resident

within me. He is there to be my helper. Why not ask His assistance concerning crucifying our old nature? I am sure He is more than willing to assist. Each morning I pray, "Dear Lord, help me even now to crucify my flesh. Help me to walk in the spirit today. Help me to live as I ought to live."

I must confess, there are often days when I must come back and "re-crucify" my flesh and seek the help of the Holy Spirit. Temptation comes, a foul attitude comes, unkind words come, or deeds arise that are not right. I must deal with these and not wait until tomorrow. Mom and Dad, teach your children to do the same. In this regard, they are no different from an adult Christian. They must deal with their flesh each day, or they will walk in the flesh that day.

8. **Keep the temptations of the world as far from your children as possible**. That, as you will remember, is called "the principle of separation." The flesh and the world are bosom buddies. They are on the same wavelength spiritually. They attract each other. There is great wisdom in keeping the world and the things of the world as far from your children as you can. The world will stimulate and promote the old nature in your children.

Actually, the underlying precept woven through this book is the matter of training our children to walk in the Spirit. It is only then that they will get the victory over the flesh. And it is only then that they will find victory over the various forms of sin that can destroy their lives. Moreover, walking in the spirit is the gateway for great spiritual growth and development. We must learn to walk in the spirit before we can run the race. It is an essential ingredient to godliness.

Conclusion

My most precious assets, apart from my salvation and my wife, are my children. They have been our life for decades. They no doubt will continue to be so. From the time they were born, we have focused on training them to serve the Lord. When they were small, we dedicated them to the Lord. The word "dedicate" literally means "to deed over." Years ago, we gave the deed to their lives to the Lord. And that has put a great responsibility upon us to train them to serve Him.

Our goal has not been to train them to excel in given areas, though they have. Our goal has not been to groom them to be popular, though in their circles they have been. Rather, our goal was to train them to be godly and to serve Jesus Christ, hopefully in full time Christian service.

Over the years in the ministry, I have met so many Christian parents whose attitude has been, "Well, I hope my kids turn out right. Some Christian kids do and some don't." Or another attitude I have perceived many times has been, "Well, as long as my kids don't wind up in jail, on drugs or pregnant, I'll be satisfied."

Both of these philosophies are likely to fail. God has not called us to bring up our children, so they just barely keep from going off into the world. He has called us to bring them up in the nurture and admonition of the Lord.

Our job is to so train our children that if God chooses, He may call them into His service. Our job is to train them to be godly and to walk in the spirit. Shoot high in the training of your children. Train them to *serve* Jesus Christ. How can we do less than dedicate them to Him and train them to serve Him completely?

God in His sovereignty may choose not to put them into full time Christian service. But such a goal and philosophy by itself can help keep them out of the corruption that is in the world. You will do your children and yourself a great favor by so training them.

In conclusion, **train your children to go to His Word day and night**. If all you glean from this book is that principle you will have accomplished a great deal. God's Word is foundational. Without that spiritual foundation, any superstructure of life will be tenuous.

Saturate their minds with the principle of righteousness. It will magnify God's blessing upon them, and it will be a shield of protection for them.

Train them to be self-disciplined in every area of their lives, especially in the matter of impelling themselves to do right. You will instill the essence of Christian character in so doing. But you also will give them a device which will enable them to excel in whatsoever they do.

Keep them from the world and the things of the world, particularly its music. You will never know how much good this will do for them. And it goes without saying that you must be consistent in your own example of separation.

And that leads us again to the principle of consistency and faithfulness. **Good training and teaching can be unraveled by the inconsistency and unfaithfulness of one Christian parent.** That is almost scary, but it is true. Train them to be godly and walk in the spirit.

Now, if you haven't quite figured it out yet, let me share with you the secret to this whole book. **Just train your children according to the basic pattern of genuine, biblical Christianity.** The issues of life *are* fundamentally spiritual. The principles of God's Word are the complete answer to the needs of the training of our children. Follow them faithfully. And may God bless you and your children.

Amen and amen!

Index